INSURANCE MARKETS

Information Problems
and
Regulation

by

David A. Lereah

PRAEGER SPECIAL STUDIES • PRAEGER SCIENTIFIC

New York • Philadelphia • Eastbourne, UK
Toronto • Hong Kong • Tokyo • Sydney

Library of Congress Cataloging in Publication Data

Lereah, David A.
  Insurance markets.

  Bibliography: p.
    1. Insurance – United States. 2. Insurance law –
United States. 3. Insurance, Accident – United States.
4. Insurance, Bank – United States. I. Title.
HG8531.L47   1985   368'.973   84-26403
ISBN 0-03-001019-5 (alk. paper)

Published in 1985 by Praeger Publishers
CBS Educational and Professional Publishing, a Division of CBS Inc.
521 Fifth Avenue, New York, NY 10175 USA

Printed in the United States of America on acid-free paper

INTERNATIONAL OFFICES

Orders from outside the United States should be sent to the appropriate address listed below. Orders from areas not listed below should be placed through CBS International Publishing, 383 Madison Ave., New York, NY 10175 USA

Australia, New Zealand
Holt Saunders, Pty, Ltd., 9 Waltham St., Artarmon, N.S.W. 2064, Sydney, Australia

Canada
Holt, Rinehart & Winston of Canada, 55 Horner Ave., Toronto, Ontario, Canada M8Z 4X6

Europe, the Middle East, & Africa
Holt Saunders, Ltd., 1 St. Anne's Road, Eastbourne, East Sussex, England BN21 3UN

Japan
Holt Saunders, Ltd., Ichibancho Central Building, 22-1 Ichibancho, 3rd Floor, Chiyodaku, Tokyo, Japan

Hong Kong, Southeast Asia
Holt Saunders Asia, Ltd., 10 Fl, Intercontinental Plaza, 94 Granville Road, Tsim Sha Tsui East, Kowloon, Hong Kong

Manuscript submissions should be sent to the Editorial Director, Praeger Publishers, 521 Fifth Avenue, New York, NY 10175 USA

To my parents and grandparents

Acknowledgments

There are two individuals who should be singled out for their considerable efforts. I owe a special debt of gratitiude to Professor Roger Sherman who reviewed carefully every page of this manuscript, from the very first working paper to this final draft form, and offered many suggestions for improvement. Special thanks are due to Keith Crocker who provided invaluable suggestions and comments as the study progressed.

While revising and expanding subsequent drafts of this study, I benefited greatly from the comments of several individuals. In particular, the comments by Wake Epps, William Johnson, and Tony Kuprianov, were quite helpful. I also thank Roger Watson and the FDIC for supplying the necessary data for this study. And special thanks to Roberta Kelly and Lorraine Kenny who had the arduous task of typing this manuscript into this final readable form.

And finally, I am indebted to my parents for their zealous support and encouragement, and to my wife Wendy for her relentless patience through what at times appeared to be a never ending process.

Of course, I alone am responsible for this final draft, and for whatever misuse I might have made of the suggestions of others.

In addition, the views expressed in this book are not necessarily those of the Federal Deposit Insurance Corporation.

Contents

List of Tables

1

Insurance Markets

INTRODUCTION

Uncertainty is common in our economic environment. Consumers during their lifetimes and firms in their everyday affairs are surrounded by innumerable risks of financial loss, and dealing with risk is an important economic problem for all market participants. It is not surprising that most consumers and firms try to avoid risk, but all risk cannot be eliminated. In some cases a market can deal effectively with residual risk by transferring it to a skilled and willing riskbearer. For example, consumers facing the possibility of financial loss can trade that possibility for a certain small financial loss. We refer to this institutional arrangement for handling risk as insurance.

Insurance is effective because professional insurers are able to pool the risk of individuals and compensate those few who suffer losses with funds collected from all. And because of the law of large numbers[1] the insurer's prediction for the group's expected financial loss is more reliable than any one individual's predictions for his own expected loss. Thus our aversion to risk plus the law of large numbers provide the raison d'etre for insurance.

Insurance protection takes many forms today. Insurance for business and industry is available for the protection of physical assets such as buildings, machinery, stock, etc., that could be wiped out by fire, explosion, windstorm or other perils of accident. Financial protection also is available against the loss of revenue of the business as the result of costly accidents. Insurance for the individual is available to

1

protect the home and personal possessions. Legal liability
protection also is available as a result of negligent acts or
from the operation of motor vehicles. These are only a handful
of the many areas of insurance protection offered.

Since insurance protection is pervasive throughout the
economy, the insurance industry has a significant impact on
most market participants in the economy, and insurance markets
touch almost all walks of economic life. Consumers and firms
alike all participate to some degree in the insurance process.
It is important that insurance markets serve society well. Today's insurance markets, however, are plagued with severe information problems. These information problems exist primarily
because of the inability of market participants to accurately
assess "risk," a crucial ingredient in the insurance process.
Information problems coupled with the many regulations imposed
by the government on insurance market participants may lead to
undesirable insurance market outcomes.

The objective of this study is to examine the behavior of
insurance markets that possess inherent information problems,
and to evaluate the effects of existing regulation. This task
of examining insurance regulation in light of current theory on
the effects of information has not yet been undertaken, yet is
very likely to yield knowledge about how best to regulate insurance markets. The study will focus on accident and bank
insurance markets. Accident insurance (property-liability) is
chosen because most research on information problems is carried
out in the context of accident insurance. Bank insurance is
studied here also because it has not yet been examined in the
context of information problems, even though it possesses them.
The reasons given for existing regulation in both markets also
are similar: to inhibit price wars and to protect firms from
bankruptcy.

ACCIDENT INSURANCE

Structure

Accident insurance serves as the primary product for the
property and liability insurance industry since the products
sold by this industry are contingent claims against accidental
property loss and liability judgments. The property-liability
industry includes automobile insurance, homeowner's insurance,
fire and marine insurance, health insurance, and various other
types. Four organizational types can be identified for the
firms selling property liability insurance in the United States
today. The most prevalent type of firm is the stock company,
which is a company owned by stockholders. Assets of such firms
account for nearly three fourths of the total assets in the
property-liability industry. Other types of firms are mutual
companies which are owned by their policyholders, a reciprocal

exchange which is a cooperative organization formed to share risks of its members, and, finally, Lloyd's Organization composed of underwriters each responsible for a portion of the insured's risks.

Accident insurance is marketed either by the agency system or through direct writing. Under the agency system agents represent a number of insurance firms in their capacity as sellers of insurance. Agents work on a commission basis. Direct writers are insurance firms that sell insurance directly, either through mail or by their own salesmen. The agency system dominates most lines of insurance with the exception of automobile insurance, which relies on direct writing.

The property-liability insurance firm is conveniently conceptualized as a levered investment trust.[2] It raises capital from an initial sale of stock and purchases (invests in) stocks and bonds. The resulting portfolio is used to support its insurance operations. An insurance firm then has two sources of income: income from the insurance process (premiums less costs of providing insurance) and income earned from its portfolio.

Although statistics are far from conclusive, the property-liability industry exhibits all the basic structural characteristics of the competitive market. A large number of insurance firms, moderate concentration ratios, low capital requirements, and no substantial barriers to entry are found to exist in the property-liability industry.[3]

Information Problems

Property and liability insurance firms operate in an environment with inherent information problems. These information problems exist primarily because firms are unable to distinguish among consumers according to their probabilities of incurring accident. The information problems can be called asymmetric because consumers know (or can more accurately assess) their own probabilities of incurring accident while firms have difficulty in making reliable assessments. These assessments are important because the task of an insurer is to select as customers those individuals whose probabilities of accident are similar to that of the risk group as a whole. There is a tendency, however, for individuals who have a greater probability of accident than the average of the group to seek insurance. This is called adverse selection, and it will lead to greater losses than are expected unless an insurer can identify the risks it is assuming. To avoid adverse selection, the insurer attempts to learn as much as possible at reasonable cost about applicants for insurance, so they can be classified into their appropriate risk groups. Thus applicants for automobile insurance are asked to provide such information as past driving violations, age, sex, and marital status. But such information is not sufficient to completely eliminate informational asymmetry and adverse selection. To improve their information, firms devise other strategies such as altering the menu of contract choices to individuals in order to induce individuals to self-select into their appropriate risk groups. Firms may also expend resources to improve on their abilities to classify risk. Asymmetric information thereby alters supply behavior in the marketplace.

Consumers may experience information problems as well. For example, in automobile insurance consumers may have poor information about availability of insurance policies, since the market offers a long and varied menu. Consumer misinformation may result in consumers purchasing the wrong insurance policies, i.e., policies that do not correspond with their riskiness. Only recently have states dealt effectively with the problem of limited information. Some states now provide information in the form of published guides on price differences for comparable policies among firms.

Regulation

The property-liability insurance industry has been subjected to an abundance of detailed government regulation. Reasons for government intervention in this industry are tied to the nature of the insurance business. Customers pay for insurance in advance (premiums), expecting insurance firms to provide services in the future.   These customers are concerned about whether or not the insurer will be able to pay claims if and when future losses occur. After all, an insurance policy is merely a promise which is of no value if the firm making it cannot keep it.   Also an insurance firm must be in a position to refund any unearned premium if customers decide to cancel insurance.   The nature of the insurance business, then, makes desirable some basis for assuring that insurers will be financially solvent so they can keep their promises. To secure a financially sound insurance industry is the primary reason for regulation.

Prior to 1944, regulation of insurance was carried out almost exclusively by the states. Only one serious challenge was made to oppose state regulation, in 1868 in the case of Paul v. Virginia. In this case, a Virginia resident representing a group of New York insurance companies refused to comply with Virginia's state law requiring licenses on the grounds that he was transacting interstate commerce and was therefore subject only to federal law. The case went to the United States Supreme Court, which held that insurance is not commerce and therefore not subject to regulation by the federal government.[4]

In 1944, in the case of the United States v. South-Eastern Underwriters Association, the Supreme Court made a complete reversal of the Paul v. Virginia decision of seventy-five years earlier, and established that insurance is commerce and that, when it is transacted across state borders, it is interstate commerce and subject to antitrust and other federal laws.[5] But in 1945 Congress yielded priority for regulation to states through the McCarren-Ferguson Act, which provided that federal regulation would be applicable only in the absence of effective state regulation. Further, the Act did not specify the type of state action that would constitute preemptive rate regulation. Thus, states were able to develop their own regulatory systems.

The National Association of Insurance Commissioners (NAIC) embraced model rate bills, called All-Industry Laws, which provided for the continued operation of rating bureaus. A rating bureau is an institution created by insurance firms to set prices and risk classifications based on the pooled cost experience of its member firms. States adopting the All-Industry Laws followed a form of rate regulation which for all practical purposes required the prior approval by government of insurance rate changes. Approvals were common for upward rate deviations but only under very limited circumstances were downward deviations approved.[6] Hence, the All-Industry Laws apparently inhibited price competition. The anti-competitive nature of the All-Industry Laws came after fierce price competition had resulted in a number of insurance company insolvencies prior to 1920. Insurance firms began to band together in rating bureaus to pool their data and fix prices, and the All-Industry Laws facilitated this price-fixing.

State regulation of the property-liability insurance business is conducted typically by the office of a state insurance commissioner. Although insurance regulation differs across states, the requirements imposed on insurance firms are similar. Insurance firms must fulfill certain capital requirements in order to obtain a license before transacting business. Their investment operations are regulated, since the solvency of an insurance firm depends partly on the nature as well as the amount of its assets. For example, investment in real estate, bonds, and corporate stock are carefully regulated. States also impose reserve requirements to ensure that services can be provided, as for unearned premiums. And, of course, insurance rates are regulated by the states. Rates charged by insurance firms must be approved by the commissioner. Finally, states also regulate the buyer side of the insurance business. For example, individuals may be required to purchase certain types of insurance by state law, such as automobile insurance, and are subject to minimum coverage requirements.

BANK INSURANCE

Structure

The main purpose of bank insurance is to insure depositors against loss from bank failures. Since transaction costs apparently prevent customers from purchasing deposit insurance individually, we consider that banks are acting as agents for their customers in purchasing insurance for them. One reason it might be economical for the bank to serve as agent is that all customers of any one bank face the same probability of bank failure. Banks thus may aggregate customers' deposits and purchase insurance for them, passing on premium costs in the prices they charge for services.

Our study will focus only on commercial and mutual savings banks and their participation in the insurance process will be examined. As of 1980 there were 15,164 commercial and mutual savings banks in the United States of which 14,758 purchased insurance.[7] The domestic assets of these insured banks totals approximately 1.68 trillion dollars.[8] Because banks hold a significant amount of society's wealth it is crucial that the banking system be kept solvent and stable, not only to protect customers' deposits but to assure a stable money supply.

Information Problems

Similar to the accident insurance market, the bank insurance market also operates in an environment with information problems. These information problems exist primarily because of the inability of insurance firms or banks to assess properly the probabilities of bank failure. More specifically, insurance firms are not able to distinguish among banks according to their probabilities of failure, and banks are not able to choose their appropriate coverage levels since they do not know their own probabilities of failure. As they lead to faulty choices of insurance protection these information problems may contribute to market problems. Moreover, severe information problems may preclude a well functioning competitive bank insurance market, and thus, they can provide a rationale for government intervention.

Regulation

The failure of more than a third of the nation's banks during the 1920's suggested a need for more soundness in the banking structure. One attempt to satisfy this need was the Banking Act of 1933, which led to the creation of the Federal Deposit Insurance Corporation (FDIC). The FDIC was established to restore public confidence in the banking system, protect depositors from deposit loss due to bank failure, and promote safe and sound banking practices. The FDIC pursues these purposes today through a program of deposit insurance covering almost 15,000 commercial and mutual savings banks and through the regulation and supervision of over 9,000 insured state-chartered banks that are not members of the Federal Reserve System.[9]

The bank insurance industry is non-competitive in that there are many buyers of insurance (commercial and mutual savings banks) but only one seller, the FDIC. The limit of FDIC deposit insurance coverage was $2,500 per depositor when deposit insurance became effective on January 1, 1934, and has been increased most recently on March 31, 1980 to $100,000 per depositor. Also, deposit insurance is mandatory for national banks and state bank members of the Federal Reserve System.

In providing deposit insurance to banks, the FDIC sets premiums at a uniform rate based on the bank's total deposits rather than its insured deposits. The FDIC charges participating banks assessments of 1/12th of one percent of their total deposits annually for the insurance it provides. The charges are returned to the institutions, less any losses paid out. As of 1980, the FDIC insurance fund totaled $11 billion.[10] The FDIC fund also is backed by statutory authority to borrow up to $3 billion from the U.S. Treasury.

The FDIC has supervisory authority over all the banks it insures. For example, the FDIC engages in bank examination and supervision with the express purpose of preventing bank failures. Further, the FDIC is empowered to facilitate merger between any bank in financial distress and a financially sound bank. And, finally, the FDIC and the Federal Reserve impose other regulations intended to preserve market stability. For example, the FDIC imposes asset restrictions on bank portfolios as an attempt to control bank riskiness. The Federal Reserve, in an attempt to inhibit 'damaging' price competition, imposes ceiling restrictions on interest rates that commercial banks may pay on time deposits, i.e., Regulation Q. The FDIC exercises the same authority over nonmember banks that participate in its deposit insurance program.

OVERVIEW OF STUDY

This study proceeds in the following steps. Chapter 2 presents a review of relevant literature. Specifically, the chapter surveys those parts of the economics of uncertainty and imperfect information which are particularly relevant for insurance markets, and then examines the behavior of the accident and bank insurance markets. Insurance market studies dealing specifically with information problems are found to be separate from insurance market studies dealing specifically with regulation. What is needed is study of regulation using methods that deal with information problems.

Chapter 3 examines today's accident insurance markets in the context of information problems. Specifically, a basic model of the accident insurance market, based on previous accident insurance models, is developed, and the effects of government intervention on insurance market outcomes are assessed. Real world observations in the property-liability

industry are then presented and contrasted with the theoreti-
cal findings.   The chapter then discusses whether government
regulations provide a useful service for society and offers
possible alternative arrangements to the present regulatory
scheme.

Chapter 4 focuses on an activity that firms participate
in when information problems exist: the classifying of individuals into their appropriate risk classes.   The objective
is to examine the role of risk classification and assess its
effects on insurance market outcomes. Specifically, the analysis compares the two risk classification schemes used today, a
rating   bureau's   classifications,   and   an   independent
firm's classifications.   The analysis then illustrates how the
use of the two classification schemes and the accuracy of the
risk classification process are affected by both competitive
and regulated insurance market environments.

Chapter 5 examines today's bank insurance market in the
context of information problems.   An examination of how market
information problems have led to the current FDIC-bank insurance market arrangement are first presented.   The chapter then
assesses FDIC regulations on bank market outcomes and presents
an alternative arrangement to the present regulatory scheme.

Chapter 6 is an empirical investigation into the possibility of commercial bank risk classification. Logit analysis is
performed on a sample of commercial banks consisting of
failed commercial banks and a representative sample of solvent commercial banks in order to estimate a vector of bank
risk characteristics.   These banks are then grouped into risk
classes based on their parameter estimates and the risk classification process is tested with a holdout sample.   Finally, a
summary and some conclusions are presented in Chapter 7.

NOTES

1.   The Law of Large numbers holds that the larger the number of observations, the more precise are estimates of the underlying (true) probability.

2.   See Joskow (53).

3.   A detailed structural study of the property-liability insurance industry can be found in Joskow (53).

4.   Paul v. Commonwealth of Virginia   75 U.S.(8 Wallace 168), 1868.

5.   United States v.   Southeastern Underwriters Association, 322 U.S. 533.

6.   Virginia   State Corporation   Commission Report (111), page 13.

7.   Federal   Deposit Insurance   Corporation 1980 annual report (30), Table 102, page 224.

8.   Ibid., page 234.

9.   In 1979, 14,758 commercial banks and mutual savings banks were   covered by deposit insurance, and   regulation and supervision was exercised over 9,336 state chartered banks that were insured but were not members of the Federal Reserve System, see the Federal Deposit Insurance Corporation 1980 annual report (30), page 3.

10.   Ibid., page 31.

2

Recent Developments
in the Industry

INTRODUCTION

The relatively recent incorporation of uncertainty and
information problems into insurance market analysis has greatly
improved our understanding of individual decision making and
market equilibrium in insurance markets. Modelling individual
and firm behavior in an uncertain environment is necessary to
represent an insurance market, since the process of insurance
arises out of uncertainty. And since insurance markets are
plagued with information problems, models incorporating imperfect information also will improve our understanding of insurance market outcomes. This chapter takes the more tractable
aim of surveying only parts of the economics of uncertainty
and imperfect information which are particularly relevant for
insurance markets.

THE ECONOMICS OF UNCERTAINTY

It is appropriate to begin with the expected utility theorem developed by John von Neumann and Oskar Morgenstern (112),
who built a theory of individual preferences among alternative
risky situations by stressing the utility resulting from each
possible outcome. They submitted certain axioms about individual behavior that implied the existence of a utility function
to represent an individual's preferences among risky alternatives. In effect, expected utility was an index that could
be assigned to any given uncertain[1] prospect. The axioms, or
"postulates of rational choice," justified the joint use of

cardinal utilities and the expected utility rule to define individuals' preferences among risky alternatives.[2]

The implications of the expected utility hypothesis can be examined with a simple example. Consider an individual who confronts an uncertain situation in which two states of the world are possible. The word "state" is defined here to mean an event with an assigned probability of occurrence. Let us assume that this uncertain situation is a lottery ticket offered to the individual with a probability p^1 that he wins R_1 dollars and a probability $p^2(=1-p^1)$ that he wins R_2 dollars, where $R_2 > R_1$. The individual derives utility $U(R_1)$ from receiving R_1 dollars and utility $U(R_2)$ from receiving R_2 dollars, where $U(R_2) > U(R_1)$. Expected utility is simply the weighted average of the utilities of the prizes R_1 and R_2 in the lottery where the weights are the respective probabilities. The expected utility, $\bar{U}$, of this lottery ticket is

(1) $$\bar{U} = p^1 U(R_1) + (1-p^1)U(R_2).$$

Assuming diminishing marginal utility of wealth, i.e., $U'' < 0$, implies that individuals are risk-averse. They will always prefer a sure bet (amount of dollars) to any lottery or prospect having the same mathematical expectation. Consider our lottery example above. The mathematical expectation of income, $\bar{R}$, from the lottery is

(2) $$\bar{R} = p^1 R_1 + (1-p^1)R_2.$$

An individual would prefer a certain payment equal to the expected value of $\bar{R}$ to any lottery ticket with expected value $\bar{R}$.

This type of behavior is called risk-aversion. It follows that risk-averse individuals provided with a sure income would never accept a fair gamble. Risk aversion is often assumed for individuals, based on the observed fact that people avoid risk.

Employing the expected utility hypothesis, individual and firm behavior in an uncertain environment can be illustrated. Arrow (4) and Debreu (25) developed models that viewed the objects of choice as contingent consumption claims. These contingent claims were "entitlements to particular commodities of commodity baskets valid only under specified states of the world."[3] Debreu treated commodities that are delivered in different states of nature as different commodities, assuming there are distinct markets for these different commodities. Claims on the commodities would be contingent on the state of nature actually occurring, and so were called contingent claims. This treatment allows us to examine market behavior under uncertainty even though complete contingent claims markets do not exist. Arrow also developed a contingent commodity model of an exchange economy.

A very simple two-state, contingent-claim model can be illustrated following the particularly simple and lucid presentation of Hirshleifer and Riley (47) rather than the original treatment of Debreu or Arrow. Consider a market where it is assumed that the uncertainty of the environment depends upon the choice that nature makes between two states of the world. Denote these two states by s_1 and s_2 with corresponding probabilities p^1 and $p^2(=1-p^1)$. In Figure 2.1 below, the commodities c_1 and c_2 on the horizontal and vertical axes represent claims to income contingent upon the occurrence of state 1 or state 2. Employing the expected utility theorem each individual has an expected utility over the commodities c_1 and c_2,

$$(3) \qquad U(c_1,c_2) = p^1U(c_1) + (1-p^1)U(c_2) \ .$$

Indifference curves in Figure 2.1 correspond to equations such as (3) where their slopes can be expressed by the marginal utilities,

$$(4) \qquad \frac{dc_2}{dc_1}\bigg|_{dU=0} = \frac{p^1U'(c_1)}{(1-p^1)U'(c_2)}$$

Now consider an individual whose initial endowment is at point E in the diagram where he claims I_1 income if state 1 occurs and I_2 income if state 2 occurs. He starts in a risky position since $I_1 \neq I_2$. Note that any point on the 45° line, which equates I_1 with I_2, represents a no-risk (certainty) position. Suppose there exists a contingent claims market such that contingent claims c_1 and c_2 can be exchanged in the price ratio π_1/π_2 where line EL' reflects this price ratio. Following standard analysis, utility maximization leads to an equilibrium position where the line EL' is just tangent to indifference curve U_1 at point e_1. At this tangency the condition

$$(5) \qquad \frac{p^1U'(c_1)}{(1-p^1)U'(c_2)} = \frac{\pi_1}{\pi_2}$$

is satisfied; the slope of the indifference curve is equal to the price ratio. Notice that the individual still remains in an uncertain situation at e_1 which is to the right of the certainty line. Only if the price ratio is fair, i.e., $\pi_1/\pi_2 = p^1/p^2$, will an individual move to the certainty line, as at point e_2 where the fair price line EL'' is tangent to indifference curve U_2. For if a fair price exists, equation (5) reduces reduces to

$$(6) \qquad \frac{U'(c_1)}{U'(c_2)} = 1$$

and assuming that utility is independent of the state,[4] equation (6) results in $c_1=c_2$.

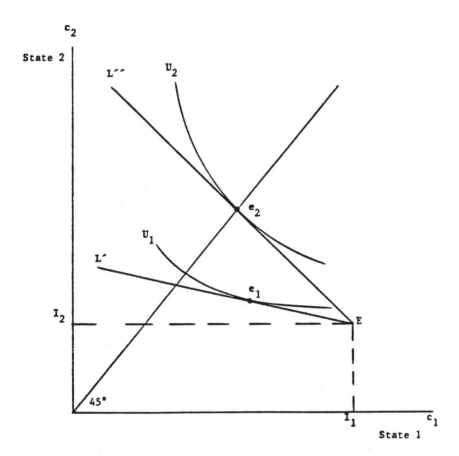

FIGURE 2.1

13

INSURANCE MARKET ANALYSIS

Traditional contingent claim models have been extended to examine accident insurance market behavior.[5] Almost all insurance market examinations since Arrow (5) have employed variants of the contingent claim model.[6] Extending the previous analysis further illustrates a simple insurance market model.

Consider, the simple two-state world described earlier in which the market for accident insurance is examined, so that s_1 and s_2 denote an accident state and no accident state with corresponding probabilities p^1 and $p^2(=1-p^1)$. To characterize demand for accident insurance assume individuals have von Neumann-Morgenstern utility functions, U, where U is twice continuously differentiable over expected wealth, $U'>0$, $U''<0$. Also assume that an individual's objective is to maximize expected utility. Suppose an individual initially has wealth W and, if the accident state occurs, he will lose L dollars.

Participating in the accident insurance market, the individual can insure himself against an accident by paying to an insurance firm a premium πq (where π is the rate of insurance per unit of coverage, q, in return for which he will be paid q dollars if an accident occurs). The individual's expected utility, EV, for this insurance arrangement is then

$$(7) \qquad EV = p^1 U(W-L-\pi q+q) + (1-p^1) U(W-\pi q)$$

where the term $(W-L-\pi q+q)$ is the individual's wealth if an accident occurs and $(W-\pi q)$ is the individual's wealth if no accident occurs. The individual's maximization problem is then to choose that amount of coverage, q^*, that maximizes his expected utility of wealth over the two states of the world. First order conditions, similar to equation (5), are

$$(8) \qquad \frac{U'(W-L+(1-\pi)q)}{U'(W-\pi q)} \; \frac{p^1}{(1-p^1)} = \frac{\pi}{1-\pi}$$

Equation (7) and the left-hand side of equation (8) yield downward sloping indifference curves similar to those in Figure 2.1 and are placed in Figure 2.2 below. Figure 2.2 depicts the accident insurance market where the horizontal axis measures wealth in the no-accident state, W_{na}, and the vertical axis measures wealth in the accident state, W_a.

Assume that insurance firms are risk neutral and are concerned only with maximizing expected profits. The supply of insurance can be characterized by noting that insurance firms receive $\pi q-q$ dollars if accident occurs and πq dollars if no accident occurs. Hence, expected profits,[7] $E\phi$, for firms

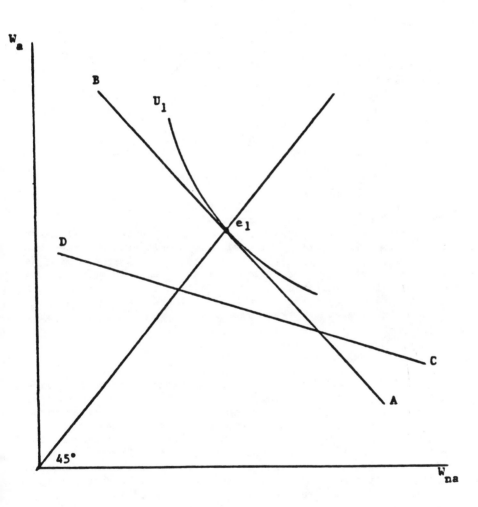

FIGURE 2.2

15

selling insurance contracts are

(9) $$E\phi = (1-p^1)\,\pi q - p^1(1-\pi)q.$$

Assuming long-run competition forces profits of insurance firms to zero, equation (9) implies that

(10) $$\frac{\pi}{1-\pi} = \frac{p^1}{1-p^1}.$$

Equation (9) yields insurance contract lines in Figure 2.2. The slope of these lines depends on the price, π, of the insurance contract. Contract line AB in Figure 2.2 represents insurance contract offerings in a competitive market, where the slope of this line reflects an actuarially fair price for insurance as determined in equation (10). Similarly, contract line CD represents a price for the insurance contract greater than what is actuarially fair.

To characterize market behavior in a competitive insurance market, simply insert (10) into the consumer's first order condition, equation (8). This results in

(11) $$U'(W-L + (1-\pi)q) = U'(W-\pi q).$$

Since individuals are strictly risk-averse, $U'' < 0$, (11) implies

(12) $$L = q.$$

Thus individuals will fully insure when faced with actuarially fair prices for insurance. Market equilibrium occurs at point e_1 in Figure 2.2 where the individual's indifference curve, U_1, is tangent to the firm's actuarially fair contract line AB at the certainty line (45° line). It is easy to show that an individual will partially insure (will be to the right of the certainty line) when faced with a price greater than is actuarially fair, e.g., contract line CD.[8]

INFORMATION PROBLEMS

Information problems exist in insurance markets primarily because of the inabilities of market participants to accurately assess risk. A relatively recent body of literature has examined accident insurance market behavior in the context of information problems.[9] This literature has stressed primarily the effects on insurance market outcomes of moral hazard, informational asymmetries, and inaccurate information. An important generality can be inferred from these studies: the conventional perfect information condition is not a good approximization for insurance market behavior.

Moral hazard results from imperfect information in that an insurance firm can not perfectly monitor the behavior of its insured customers. For an insurance firm, the cost of providing its product (an insurance contract) depends on the behavior of the purchaser. For example, an individual can increase or decrease his risk of incurring an automobile accident by increasing or decreasing the number of miles driven per year. If an insurance firm cannot perfectly monitor the behavior of its customers, the price it sets for insurance will not be directly related to its costs. Although the resulting problem for the firm is widely known as the moral hazard problem, Pauly (83,84) has pointed out that the consumer's action is purely rational and should not really be viewed as a moral issue. A brief description of Pauly's analysis (84) illustrates what is still known as the moral hazard problem.

Pauly extends the two-state accident insurance model outlined earlier by allowing individuals to engage in loss-prevention acitivities, Z, which reduce the probability, p of the dollar loss, L, associated with accident. By making p a function of Z and also recognizing that loss-prevention activities, Z, are a cost and detract from individual wealth, equation (7) is altered and becomes the individual's expected utility of wealth in equation (13) below,

$$(13) \qquad p(Z)U(W-Z-L-\pi q+q) \; + \; (1-p(Z)U(W-Z-\pi q).$$

Assuming the premium πq is independent of Z, Pauly demonstrates that competitive equilibrium leads to an over-production of insurance and an under-use of preventive activity (an increase in moral hazard).

Much of the recent work in insurance market behavior is in the context of informational asymmetries.[10] However, the primary purpose of most of these works is to develop further our understanding of the effects of imperfect information on market outcomes and not to examine insurance markets in their own right. Since insurance markets possess inherent information problems, they afford an ideal place to examine informational asymmetries.[11]

Asymmetric information in an insurance market exists when firms are unable to distinguish among consumers according to their probabilities of incurring accident. Two serious problems may arise. First, a market may not exist in the conventional sense in which firms set price and allow consumers to choose coverage levels. Second, adverse selection may result because high-risk individuals will try to obtain contracts intended for low-risk individuals.

The first problem can be illustrated through a simple example.[12] Consider an accident insurance market in which there are two states, accident and no accident, and two types of individuals, high-risk and low-risk individuals, with corresponding probabilities of incurring accident p^H and p^L. Assume that each risk group is of the same size and faces the same loss, L. Also assume that asymmetric information exists in

that firms are not able to distinguish between low- and high-
risk groups. The price for insurance, π^*, is set actuarially
fair for the entire population of individuals, i.e., it corresponds to the expected probability of loss for the population
($p^* = (p^H + p^L)/2$. Figure 2.3 below depicts the ensuing market
problem.   The vertical axis measures the price for insurance,
π^*, and the horizontal axis measures coverage, q.   Low-risk
and high-risk groups' demand curves, D^L and D^H are functions
of price, π and riskiness, p, and are placed in the diagram.
Notice that riskiness is a shift variable so that D^H is to the
right of D^L.   Since firms offer insurance to both groups at
price π^*, the low risk group purchases q^L coverage and the
high-risk group purchases q^H coverage.   Thus a firm's expected
losses, the rectangle $p^H cd\pi^*$, are greater than expected gains,
rectangle $\pi^* abp^L$. Hence the notion of a conventional price and
quantity insurance market may fail to exist when the market exhibits asymmetric information.[13]

Much of the recent work on problems of informational
asymmetries in insurance markets are extensions of the model of
Rothschild and Stiglitz (93) model who constructed a two state
(accident, no accident) insurance market similar to the model
developed earlier which demonstrates the problems of adverse
selection.   Individuals participating in the insurance process
then choose coverage by maximizing their expected utility of
wealth,

(13) $EU = pU(W-L-\pi q+q) + (1-p)U(W-\pi q),$

and risk neutral firms offer insurance contracts based on their
expected profits, $E\phi$,

(14) $E\phi = (1-p)\pi q - p(1-\pi)q.$

If firms offer actuarially fair prices in a competitive insurance arrangement, individuals will fully insure, so that L = q.

This model is further extended by assuming that there are
two groups of individuals, high and low risk groups, with corresponding probabilities of accident, p^H and p^L.   Each risk
group is of the same size and faces the same loss, L.

Outcomes in a competitive market with no asymmetric information or adverse selection are illustrated in Figure 2.4
below. Assume both low and high risk individuals start with an
initial endowment (W-L,W) at point E in an uninsured state.
The set of contracts offered by a firm for low-risk individuals
which just breaks even is given by equation (14) where p^L is
substituted for p, and is depicted in Figure 2.4 by the line
EL. Similarly, the set of contracts offered by a firm for high
risk individuals is given by line EH. The slopes of both lines
reflect the price of insurance for each risk group, π^L for the
low risk group and π^H for the high risk group.   Indifference
curves for low and high risk groups are derived from the first

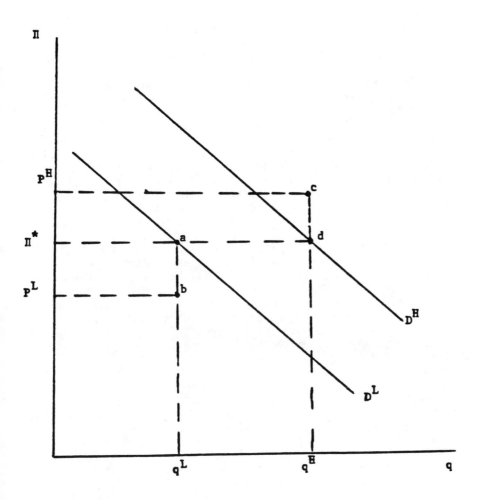

FIGURE 2.3

19

order conditions of (13) substituting the appropriate p's, and they are placed in Figure 2.4 as U^L and U^H respectively. Assuming perfect information and actuarially fair prices, market equilibrium results in firms offering, and low and high risk groups purchasing, full coverage contracts α^L and α^H respectively.

When asymmetric information exists, because firms are not able to differentiate between low and high risk individuals, adverse selection problems may arise. If firms were to offer contracts α^L and α^H, high risk individuals would no longer be content with α^H, since α^L offers more wealth in both states of the world. High risk individuals would naturally choose α^L instead, to reach a higher indifference curve. If firms are not able to distinguish a high risk from a low risk individual then both high and low risk individuals purchase α^L. Firms would then lose money. Thus (α^L, α^H) is not an equilibrium. In a Nash equilibrium each firm is assumed to determine the set of contracts it will offer under the assumption that all other firms make no changes in their current offerings. Indeed, the only set of contracts satisfying this condition is $(\alpha^H, \alpha^{L'})$ in Figure 2.4. An offer of these contracts will keep high risk individuals at α^H, since $\alpha^{L'}$ is on U^H. Low risk individuals will move to $\alpha^{L'}$, where they consume less than full coverage. Thus low risk individuals can signal their 'quality' to firms by their willingness to purchase an inexpensive low coverage contract while high risk individuals signal their high riskiness by purchasing expensive high coverage contracts.[14]

The existence of the separating Nash equilibrium $(\alpha^H, \alpha^{L'})$ depends on the proportion of high risk individuals in the market and an equilibrium may not exist at all. This argument is illustrated in Figure 2.5 below. Recall that the Nash separating equilibrium for contract lines EL and EH is $(\alpha^H, \alpha^{L'})$. However, if line EF represents the market fair odds line of low and high risk individuals in the market, the separating equilibrium $(\alpha^H, \alpha^{L'})$ will not exist. To see this, notice that the low risk individual's indifference curve, U^L, through point α^L_1, lies below the market fair odds line EF. Thus there exists a pooling contract γ, preferred by both low- and high-risk individuals, which makes positive profits if $(\alpha^H, \alpha^{L'})$ is offered. Hence, $(\alpha^H, \alpha^{L'})$ is not a Nash equilibrium. Further, a pooling Nash equilibrium also cannot exist. Consider the pooling contract β on the market fair odds line EF. Low and high risk individual indifference curves U^L_2 and U^H_2 passing through point β are placed in the diagram. Since U^L_2 is flatter than U^L_2 (see equation (4)) there exists a contract λ that is preferred by low-risk individuals to contract β, so some insurance firm can be expected to offer it and attract low-risk customers. As low-risk individuals leave contract β, firms offering β incur losses since they serve only high-risk customers. Eventually firms do not offer contract β so that high-risk individuals then purchase contract λ which then ultimately losses money. Thus a pooling Nash equilibrium does not exist. Rothschild and

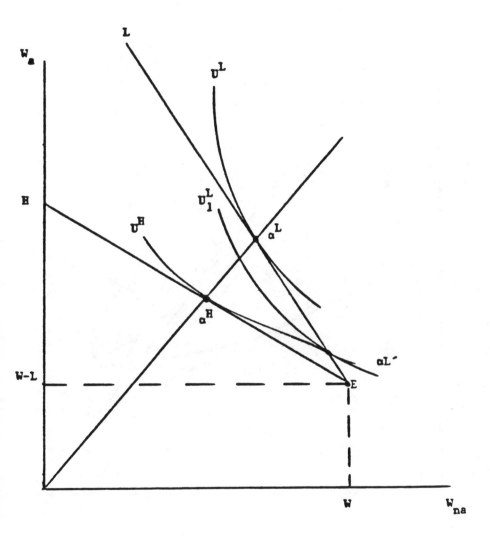

FIGURE 2.4

21

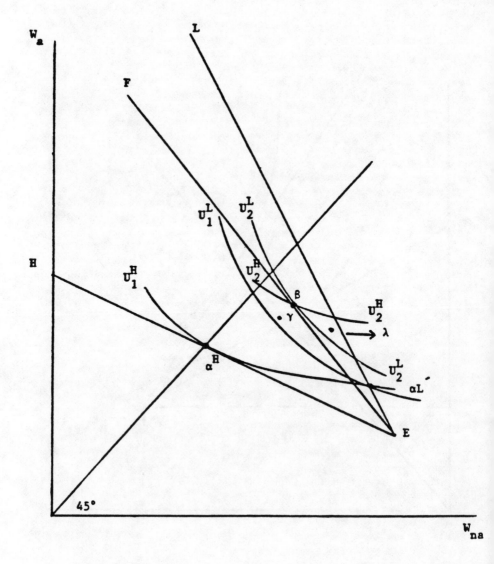

FIGURE 2.5

22

Stiglitz conclude that if the proportion of low-risk individuals is sufficiently high a Nash equilibrium may not exist.

Wilson (113), utilizing a different definition of equilibrium, demonstrates that a pooling equilibrium may exist even when a separating equilibrium does not. A Wilson equilibrium involves some foresight on the part of each firm. In a Wilson equilibrium the optimal set of policies offered by each firm is determined under the assumption that any currently marketed policies which become unprofitable as a result of their new offerings will no longer be offered. Thus in Figure 2.5, the pooling contract β is a Wilson equilibrium since firms are assumed to have the foresight to know that the offerings of contracts such as λ eventually lead to unprofitable outcomes and thus they do not offer such contracts.

Spence (103) extends the works of Rothschild and Stiglitz (93) and Wilson (113)[15] by recognizing that markets with informational asymmetries respond by "implicitly maximizing the benefits to low-risk people subject to the constraints imposed by the informational asymmetries."[16] Spence employs a more elaborate equilibrium concept than do Rothschild and Stiglitz or Wilson. In a Spence equilibrium, firms offer an array of policies where some policies may subsidize other policies. Under such a scheme, some policies might incur losses while others earn profits on the condition that the total array of policies do not incur losses.

Briefly stated, for the two-risk-group case, Spence develops a model in which a firm's objective function consists of maximizing low risk individual's utility subject to the constraints that the high-risk group is at least as well-off and that the firm just breaks even. Generalizing to the n-group case, he develops a more elaborate objective function in which its structure is closely related to the two-group case. From the model he concludes that the highest risk group receives an optimal amount of coverage while all other risk groups receive somewhat less than optimal coverage.

Kleindorfer and Kunreuther (59) and Hoy (49) examine insurance market behavior in the presence of inaccurate information. Kleindorfer and Kunreuther's work examines consumer and firm inaccuracies in assessing consumer risk and how these informational flaws affect market outcomes. Their analysis takes place within a Rothschild and Stiglitz two-state world in which consumer and firm misperceptions about consumer risk are examined. The primary interest of their study is how these misperceptions affect the stability of Nash and Wilson equilibriums. For example, they conclude that in the case where firms correctly perceive consumer risk, consumer misperceptions result in welfare losses only when they underestimate the risk involved and purchase less insurance then they would have if perfectly informed. Other conclusions also are presented for many possible combinations of consumer and firm misperceptions in a Nash and Wilson equilibrium setting.

Hoy (49) examines the effects of 'imperfectly categorizing risks' on market outcomes in the Rothschild-Stiglitz two-state world. Firms engage in risk categorization in order to improve on their ability to identify individuals (i.e., low and high risk) in the market.   Hoy's contribution can be easily illustrated in Figure 2.6 below.   Figure 2.6 depicts the usual accident, no accident type world containing low-and high-risk groups with a market fair odds line EF and group fair odds lines for low and high risk consumers EL and EH respectively. Imperfect categorization divides the market fair odds line into two pooled lines EF´ and EF´´.   Line EF´ is to the right of line EF since it is comprised of mostly low risk individuals but contains some high risk individuals because of imperfect categorization.   Similarly, line EF´´ lies to the left of line EF.   Hoy demonstrates from a Wilson equilibrium, i.e., W, imperfect categorization has ambiguous welfare effects resulting in the set of contracts (c_1, c_2).   Some individuals are made better off going from W to c_1 while some individuals are made worse off going from W to c_2.   However, from an initial separating equilibrium, i.e., (α^H, α^L), imperfect categorization unambiguously improves welfare resulting in the contract c_1 offered to the 'perceived' low risk group and the separating contract $(\alpha^H, \alpha^{L´})$ offered to the remaining 'perceived' high risk individuals.   Thus, Hoy concludes that imperfectly categorizing risks leads to a Pareto improvement in welfare only when the initial equilibrium is of the Nash separating type.

ACCIDENT INSURANCE REGULATION

There has been a great deal of interest in the effects of regulation on both firm and consumer in many industries since the work of Averch and Johnson (9).   However, despite abundant government regulation of the property-liability (P-L) insurance industry, prior to 1973, P-L regulation studies were confined to state and federal insurance commissions and the like.   Joskow's work (53) was the first attempt to examine the workings of the P-L insurance industry and the effects of insurance regulation in an industrial organization context. With the exception of Joskow and a few others,[17] studies in insurance regulation are still products of state and federal insurance commissions.

Joskow (53) provides a detailed study of the workings of the P-L insurance industry.   The study concludes that the P-L industry "possesses the structural characteristics normally associated with the idealized competitive market: a large number of firms, operating in a market with low concentration levels, selling essentially identical products, provided at constant unit costs, and with ease of entry of new and potential competitors."[18]   Joskow demonstrates, however, that pervasive state regulation results in a movement away from competitive

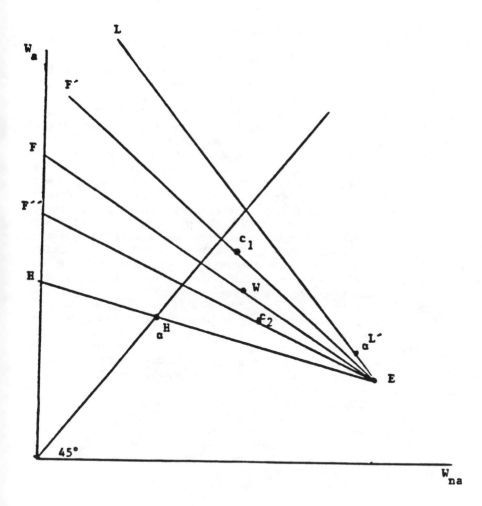

FIGURE 2.6

25

behavior. The study cites the use of an inefficient sales
technique (the agency system), limited availability of insurance for high risk individuals, and over-capitalization.
To assist in his examination, Joskow develops a model of a P-L
insurance firm incorporating the investment side of the firm as
well as its insurance operations. Even though the model neglects explicitly to incorporate consumer behavior and imperfect
information, it is an important step in assessing rate regulation on insurance market behavior.

Saba (94) presents empirical evidence that the behavior of
insurance firms is consistent with a model of an insurance
market where the regulated rate is fixed above the competitive
rate. Simply stated, if the regulated rate is above the competitive rate, we should expect to find firms operating away
from the minimum point on their average cost curves. Saba
demonstrates, for the automobile insurance market, that rate
regulation results in firms operating to the left of the minimum point of their average cost curves. He then concludes that
regulated rates are fixed above their competitive counterparts.

Munch and Smallwood's works present an examination of
solvency regulation of the P-L insurance industry. Their first
paper (79) is concerned primarily with the cost and benefits of
solvency regulation. They develop an analysis which employs the
capital asset pricing model to describe an insurance firm's
behavior. They then examine the effects of solvency regulation
on firm behavior, recognizing that consumers may not be able to
distinguish financial stability among different firms. Besides
losses of policyholders if a firm becomes insolvent the firm's
owners also lose their equity.[19] Munch and Smallwood (80) also
present empirical evidence concerning the effects of solvency
regulation on insurance firms. They conclude that minimum
capital requirements reduce insolvencies by reducing the number
of small firms. However, conclusions on the effects of other
solvency regulations cannot be reached.

In an enlightening study, MacAvoy (68) examines federal-
state regulation on the pricing and marketing of insurance, and
questions the efficiency of insurance regulation in the P-L
industry. By examining the behavior of eleven insurance firms
in a competitive state, California, and two regulated states,
New Jersey and Pennsylvania, the study reaches some interesting
conclusions about the effects of regulation and offers a
proposal on insurance reform. Briefly, the study reports that
rate regulation "discourages rate reductions, contributes to
instability in insurance company operations, establishes various forms of cross-subsidization between good and bad risks,
imposes unnecessary restrictions on the collective merchandis-
ing and the direct writing of insurance, and aggravates the
availability problem in which marginal or high risks have
difficulty obtaining coverage in the open market at the pre-
vailing rates."[20] The study then submits recommendations
for regulatory reform. The basic thrust of its proposal is to

create a dual system of regulation of insurance similar to the bank regulatory system. The proposal suggests that an agency similar to the Federal Deposit Insurance Corporation for banks guarantee insurance firm solvency. Insurance firms would then have the option of seeking federal charter and thus be subject to federal control, or retain their state status and remain subject to state regulation. In this way, firms have the option to participate in a competitive system or stay with state regulation.

It was the intention of the last sections of this review to summarize current research in the accident insurance market. The survey was intended to examine the effects of information problems on market outcomes and to present studies concerned with the assessment of accident insurance regulation. Studies dealing specifically with information problems are separate from regulatory studies. What is needed is study of regulation using methods that deal with information problems. Information studies in their own right already have contributed significantly to our understanding of accident insurance markets and how they behave for different information problems. And in discussing the implications of their models, most of these studies offer suggestions for government intervention. A study that assesses insurance regulations in the context of information problems, then, seems appropriate.

BANK INSURANCE MARKET STUDIES

The bank insurance market literature is now surveyed. Of particular concern is bank insurance market behavior, the effects of information problems on market outcomes, and assessments of Federal Deposit Insurance Corporation (FDIC) deposit insurance. This review confines its attention to those studies concerned with the federal deposit insurance system which began in 1933. It was this year that marked the beginning of a formal bank insurance market, a consequence of the creation of the FDIC.[21] Since its beginning, the insurance system has kept intact in that there has been no fundamental structural change.[22] Further, "there has been little public debate over the workings of the existing system."[23] However, there have been some attempts to examine bank insurance in the literature.[24] The primary focus of these studies is on bank insurance market behavior and assessments of FDIC regulations. Unfortunately, these examinations are not made in the context of information problems.

For expositional purposes, this review is divided into three topics: assessments of the deposit insurance market, the FDIC-bank failure relationship, and deposit insurance and regulations. Only studies associated with the latter topic explicitly model deposit insurance behavior.

Assessments of Deposit Insurance

Early deposit insurance studies present discussions on the
'current state of deposit insurance' and then offer proposals
on regulatory reform. Most studies conclude that the FDIC
insurance system has been successful in preventing bank panics
and thus it promotes a sound banking system. However, these
studies also recognize that the FDIC has produced several
disturbing side effects. Basing insurance premiums on total
deposits rather than insured deposits produces an inefficiency
in the system. Large depositors end up subsidizing small
depositors and they are also ineligible for full coverage
offered small depositors. Also the price of these deposit-
based premiums are set too high since the FDIC reserve it produces is more than enough to cover annual FDIC losses in any
year since 1943. "It is clear from the growth of the insurance
reserve that the premiums charged by the FDIC since its es-
tablishment are in excess of those required to cover the risks
of normal failures, i.e., the sort of failures that have been
experienced."[25]
Scott and Mayer (96) also argue that insurance premiums
have forced banks to pay more of the costs of bank failures
than they have generated. They suggest that "banks should only
cover losses attributable to fraud, misconduct and normal
managerial failure."
Most studies propose that all deposits be fully insured
because of the stated inequities and premium assessments should
be somehow related to bank risk. In particular, Gibson (37)
proposes that the FDIC insure against normal failures while the
Federal Reserve would insure against depression failures. In
this way, the FDIC premium would be smaller and more in tune
with bank risk.

FDIC-Bank Failure Relationship

Its obvious that the relationship between the FDIC and
bank failure is critical, since the primary objectives of the
FDIC are to promote a sound banking system and to protect the
nation's money supply. Indeed, "the primary function of
deposit insurance is, and always has been, protection of the
circulating medium from the consequences of bank failures.
That insurance also serves the purpose of guarding the small
depositor against loss from bank failure cannot be denied, but
this function is of secondary importance,"[26] Barnett, Horvitz,
and Silverberg (10) evaluate the deposit insurance system with
references to how the FDIC deals with bank failures. They note
that only small banks failed (50 million in deposits or less)
between 1934-1970 while many large banks failed (over 50
million in deposits) during the 1971-1977 period and hence
a reconsideration of the FDIC insurance system is warranted.

A discussion on the costs and benefits of 100 percent deposit insurance follows and leaves the reader with no firm commitment one way or the other on whether 100 percent deposit insurance should be imposed. They correctly suggest that there is in effect 100 percent insurance for large banks but not small banks in that "there is never a payout of a large bank with losses to uninsured depositors, whereas we have had such treatment of small bank failures.[27]

Gilbert (38) and Varvel (110) in Federal Reserve bulletin reviews, both examine policy toward bank failures. Both studies cite the increase in number and size of bank failures in recent years, in particular the two largest bank failures up to the time of their studies; the U.S. National Bank of San Diego, $934 million in deposits and Franklin National Bank of New York, $1.7 billion in deposits.[28] Gilbert notes that the recent relaxation of some recent banking regulations, which gives banks greater flexibility to respond to changing market conditions, may lead banks to "assume greater risks and hence increase their vulnerability to failure."[29] He suggests that if deposit insurance premiums are based on bank risk, this problem would be somewhat alleviated. Varvel gives attention to the activities of the FDIC in providing assistance to insolvent banks. He cites four alternative procedures that the FDIC has followed to aid insolvent banks: direct payment of insured deposits, deposit assumption, i.e., facilitating a merger with another bank, supplying direct loans to the ailing bank, and operating a deposit insurance national bank for a maximum of two years. He then examines how these alternatives were used during recent bank failures.

Deposit Insurance and Regulation

The rationale given for government regulation in the banking industry traditionally has been attributed to the protection of the nation's money supply via a sound banking system. Since the FDIC plays a major role in creating and implementing these regulations, an assessment of its role is vital not only to understanding the bank insurance market but to aid in our examination of the bank industry as well. There have been relatively recent attempts at examining bank insurance and regulation and each study is described accordingly.

Kreps and Wacht's paper (62) basically discusses the possible overlap of regulations imposed on banks. More specifically, they recognize that traditional regulations such as portfolio prohibitions, limitations of interest payments on deposits, and minimum capital requirements are attempts to assure a sound banking system, while concurrently, FDIC deposit insurance is also an attempt to promote banking stability. Simply stated, they ask whether traditional bank regulation may now be redundant. In other words, if FDIC deposit regulation

is effective, traditional restrictive regulations may be unnecessary. Their analysis considers one of these possible
overlaps: the imposition of minimum capital adequacy for banks
vis a vis FDIC deposit insurance.

Kreps and Wacht assert that the "process of supervisory
imposition of minimum standards of capital adequacy on banks,
restricts bank management's freedom of action in making important portfolio policy decisions. Banks, as profit-seeking
businessmen, ought to be free to make such decisions independent of regulation."[30] Moreover, "the effect of imposing
supervisory standards of minimum capital adequacy on banks,
to help provide maximum safety for deposits' funds, seems to be
in the direction of forcing bank management to minimize instead
of attempting to maximize, their stockholders' wealth."[31] They
argue that minimum capital standards should be replaced by
market-determined standards of minimum capital adequacy and
that any increase in bank portfolio risk as a result of lifting
the minimum capital standards, would not necessarily result
in any loss of public confidence in banks since they impose
the standards. To support their proposal, they claim that
depositors are able to evaluate the 'risks of using alternative
depository institutions.'[32]

Koehn (61) presents an examination of the effects of
solvency constraints and regulations on depository intermediary
risk and the probability of insolvency. He finds that high
capital standards may actually increase bank portfolio risk
rather than inhibit portfolio risk as claimed by Kreps and
Wacht. His analysis implies that capital standards may severe-
ly limit the amount of leverage in a bank's portfolio which may
result in lower returns on capital that may create difficulties
for the bank in attracting new capital. The bank then may purchase a riskier portfolio to offset the loss in revenue caused
by capital adequacy standards. Thus capital adequacy requirements may be counter-productive, as they may actually increase
the riskiness of a bank.

Koehn also demonstrates that asset restrictions as an
attempt to inhibit bank riskiness may promote excessive risk
taking. For example, some FDIC restrictions limit the quantity
of funds a bank may allocate to a single asset, to limit the
amount of capital exposed to any one borrower. Koehn demonstrates that this type of restriction will alter the efficient
portfolio frontier, making bank portfolios riskier. "Indeed,
because asset restrictions reduce portfolio diversification
possibilities, depository intermediaries may be unable to hold
a less risky portfolio. Intermediaries are therefore faced
with a risk-return trade-off that may be unfavorable relative
to an unconstrained situation; every point on their investment-
possibilities frontier may be worse-off or less efficient then
the unconstrained frontier (that is, the expected return for
any given level of risk is lower)."[33] Consequently, asset
restrictions may result in higher deposit risk.

Kareken and Wallace (56) examine the effects of various regulations and FDIC insurance equilibrium outcomes in the banking industry. They develop a model of bank behavior using state-preference theory and several critical assumptions. Two of their important conclusions are: (1) banks hold as risky a portfolio as regulations allow under FDIC deposit insurance if the insurance premium is independent of bank risk, and (2) capital requirements alone have little effect on bankruptcy.

Buser, Chen, and Kane (19) view their model as a generalization of the Kareken and Wallace paper. They see the FDIC as a firm selling two products, insurance and regulation, and setting two prices accordingly. Their hypothesis is that the FDIC "deliberately sets its explicit insurance premium below market value to entice state-chartered nonmember banks to submit themselves voluntarily to FDIC regulatory domain."[34] Buser, Chen, and Kane also examine the effects of deposit insurance and capital regulation (an implicit premium) on the value of the banking firm, and conclude that the FDIC base their insurance premiums on bank risk if the implicit (FDIC regulations) as well as explicit (premiums) prices for insurance are considered. They suggest that the FDIC has a risk-rated structure of implicit premium of which capital adequacy standards emerge as the critical element.

SUMMARY

This literature review prompts several comments. First, the literature has made strong advances in modelling insurance market behavior in the context of information problems. Indeed, the incorporation of uncertainty and information problems in insurance market analysis has helped improve our understanding of insurance market outcomes. Second, unfortunately, attempts to examine today's insurance markets and their regulations are made without consideration to how market participants react to information problems. And, finally, there exists no rigorous treatment of bank insurance behavior in the context of information problems.

NOTES

1. For our purposes an uncertain prospect is a probability distribution. We choose not to make a distinction between risk and uncertainty and will use the words interchangeably. However, Knight (60), offers a true distinction. He defines risk as a situation where results of actions are predictable in a probability sense. An uncertain situation has no probability distribution available for aid in prediction.

2. The literature has developed these axioms in a number of ways (for example, see Friedman and Savage (35); Herstein and Milnor (45); Markowitz (69); and Marschak (70). Luce and Raiffa (66), in particular, offer a lucid presentation of six axioms of rational behavior under uncertainty.

3. Hirshleifer and Riley (47), page 1376.

4. The utility attached to wealth may vary with the state of the world. This is called state-dependent utility. A discussion of this concept can be found in Cook and Graham, 1977(20).

5. It seems appropriate here to mention that the literature review that follows in this section and the next will focus primarily on reviewing accident insurance studies in the context of uncertainty and information problems.

6. See for example Arrow (6), Erlich and Becker (13), and Rothschild and Stiglitz (93).

7. This result would be more complicated if we assumed that insurance firms were risk averse, because they would not be concerned only with expected profits then.

8. See the Appendix B of Chapter 3 for further analysis of this case.

9. See For example, Arrow (6), (7); Pauly (83); Zeckhauser (114); Spence and Zeckhauser (96); Pauly (84); Rothschild and Stiglitz (93); Wilson (113); Spence (103); Kleindorfer and Kunreuther (59); and Hoy (49).

10. See Rothschild and Stiglitz (93).

11. There is another body of literature, however, that examines the theory of informational asymmetries generally, and in other market settings. We do not have the space adequately to review all of this literature, and only offer a brief list of some of the important works: Akerlof (1); Crocker (21); Diamond (26); Harris and Townsend (44); Grossman, S. (42); Grossman, H. (41); Grossman and Stiglitz (43); Jovanovic (54); Kihlstrom and Mirman (57); Leland and Pyle (64); Miyazaki (77); Prescott and Townsend (86); Rothschild (92); Riley (90); Salop and Salop (95); Spence (102).

12. The following exposition is based on one similar to Kleindorfer and Kunreuther (59). However, Kleindorfer and Kunreuther interpret the exposition of this problem to describe adverse selection. We shall define adverse selection in terms of the Rothschild and Stiglitz problem that immediately follow.

13. Rothschild and Stiglitz (93) suggest insurance firms offer policies which set both price and coverage in order to circumvent this problem. Their analysis of adverse selection,

which follows, employs this contract arrangement.

14. This statement makes sense if we recognize that the marginal loss in utility with purchasing less than full coverage is greater for high risk individuals since they possess higher probabilities of incurring accident.

15. Spence, in fact, generalized the work of Miyazaki (77) who demonstrated that Wilson's work was a solution to a constrained optimization problem. Miyazaki examined the labor market to develop this analysis.

16. Spence (103), page 428.

17. See for example Saba (94), Hill (46), Munch and Smallwood (79), and MacAvoy (68).

18. Joskow (53), page 391.

19. The model developed is a starting point for assessing solvency regulation; however, some (Kunreuther (63) and Lynch (67)) strongly object to the appropriateness of employing the capital asset pricing model.

20. MacAvoy (68), page 89.

21. Prior to 1933, there existed some state bank insurance systems. See Friedman and Schwartz (36).

22. The only major changes in the system have been periodic increases in deposit coverage.

23. Barnett, Horvitz, and Silverberg, 1977 (10), page 304.

24. For examples see Golembe (39); Mayer (71); Randall (88); Scott and Mayer (96); Kreps and Wacht (62); Gibson (27); Horvitz (48); Friedman and Formuzis (34); Gilbert (38); Meltzer (73); Barnett, Horvitz, and Silverberg (10); Sharpe (97); Merton (75); Kareken and Wallace (56); Blair and Heggestande (15); Buser, Chen, and Kane (19).

25. Barnett, Horvitz, and Silverberg 1977 (10), page 304.

26. Golembe (39), page 194.

27. Barnett, Horvitz, and Silverberg (10), page 331.

28. The failure of the U.S. National Bank of San Diego in 1973 was due to improper (illegal) actions by bank management e.g., management concealed the true financial condition of the bank. With the assistance of the FDIC, Crocker National Bank took full control of all of its branches. The failure of the Franklin National Bank of New York, in 1974, was due to high loan losses and especially large losses in foreign exchange transactions. Eventually with the aid of the FDIC, the European-American Bank and Trust Company assumed control of all of its 104 branches.

29. Gilbert (38), page 7.

30. Kreps and Wacht (62), page 606.

31. Ibid, page 609.

32. However, many dispute this claim (e.g., see Munch and Smallwood (79), and Kunreuther (63).

33. Koehn (61), page 2.

34. Buser, Chen, and Kane (19), page 52. However, this assertion is contrary to other works (i.e., Gibson (37) and Scott and Mayer (96)).

3

Accident Insurance

INTRODUCTION

Insurance firms and their customers in the accident insurance market operate in an environment with inherent information
problems. And as Chapter 2 reveals, both firm and customer
responses to information problems are significant in that they
directly affect insurance market outcomes. For example, insurance firms, when faced with adverse selection problems, offer
a menu of policies that induce customers to select themselves
into different groups (the market result is called a separating
equilibrium). Low-risk individuals can signal their quality
to firms by their willingness to purchase an inexpensive low
coverage contract, while high-risk individuals signal their
high riskiness by purchasing expensive high coverage contracts.
And if a separating equilibrium does not exist, firms are
forced to pool low and high risk groups and offer a pooling
contract (a pooling equilibrium). Market participants' responses to information problems suggest, then, that it is
important to assess the workings of insurance markets in the
context of information problems.

This chapter examines today's accident insurance
markets in the context of information problems. Of particular
concern is how government intervention affects market outcomes.
Specifically, the question of whether government interference
improves or aggravates government-free market outcomes is
addressed. A discussion on whether today's government regulations provide a useful service for society is then offered. It
is recognized that, basically, reasons for regulation are tied
to the nature of the insurance business which makes desirable

some basis for assuring that insurers will be financially
solvent so they can keep their promises made to customers.
The discussion, then, emphasizes the importance to secure a
financially sound insurance industry.

Two important government interferences in the accident insurance market, insurance rate regulation and minimum
insurance coverage requirements, are examined. Insurance rate
regulation is chosen because it is the most prominent type of
insurance regulation and recently has received a great deal of
attention.[1] The analyses demonstrate that rate regulation may
disturb the insurance market's way of dealing with information
problems. Indeed, rate regulation may alter a market's policy
offerings in that firms may switch from offering pooling contracts to offering separating contracts or vice versa, depending on the riskiness composition of individuals in the market.
And in some cases, rate regulation impairs a firm's ability to
respond to and even to detect changing market conditions which
may result in less stable firm operations. Minimum insurance
coverage requirements are chosen because it is a good example
of government interference on the buyer side. Coverage restrictions, when binding, may indirectly force firms to drop
their separating contracts in favor of pooling contracts. The
possibility that consumers have poor information about the
availability of insurance policies is also discussed. Incorporating this possibility with other information problems
(i.e., informational asymmetries) in insurance markets leads to
interesting results. For example, firms may take advantage of
consumer misinformation by altering coverage levels, the type
of policies offered, and the price charged for insurance
coverage. And a bias may exist in that firms will lower policy
coverage levels but will not raise them in response to consumer
misinformation.

The analysis follows the insurance market literature in
that the exposition is primarily graphical and of the
Rothschild-Stiglitz variety. Focus is only on the insurance
process (the offering and purchasing of insurance) and the investment side of insurance (firms' investment portfolios) is
ignored.[2] Also moral hazard problems and administrative costs
are assumed away for simplicity of exposition.[3] Finally,
assessments of regulatory effects on insurance market outcomes
are made from the vantage points of both the separating and
pooling equilibriums.[4]

The chapter proceeds in the following steps. The first
part presents a model of the accident insurance market which
combines the graphical techniques developed in Rothschild and
Stiglitz (93) with an equilibrium concept employed in Wilson
(113). Hence, the accident insurance market model presented is
called a Rothschild-Stiglitz-Wilson model, and hereafter
conveniently called the R-S-W model. The R-S-W model developed demonstrate the government-free separating and pooling
equilibriums. The chapter then examines the effects of rate

rate regulation and minimum insurance coverage requirements on insurance market outcomes. The problems of consumer mis-information on the availability of insurance policies are also examined. In addition, an attempt to relate real world observations in the accident insurance industry to the findings of the analyses is made. Finally, a discussion on the merits of government regulation and possible alternative arrangements to the present regulatory scheme is offered.

THE R-S-W ACCIDENT INSURANCE MODEL

Consider a simple two-state world in which the market for accident insurance is examined, so that a and na denote an accident state and no-accident state with corresponding probabilities p^1 and $p^2(=1-p^1)$. To characterize demand for accident insurance, assume individuals have von Neumann-Morgenstern utility functions, U, where U is twice continuously differentiable over expected wealth, $U'>0$, $U''<0$. Also assume an individual's objective is to maximize expected utility. Suppose individuals can be divided into two groups which differ only on the probability of their having an accident, the low-risk individuals having accident probability p^L and the high-risk individuals having accident probability p^H, where $p^H > p^L$. Further suppose that each risk group is of the same size, possesses the same initial wealth, W, and faces the same loss, L, if the accident state occurs. Participating in the accident insurance market, low-risk individuals can insure themselves against an accident by paying to an insurance firm a premium $\pi^L q$ (where π^L is the low-risk rate of insurance per unit of coverage, q) in return for which they will be paid q dollars if an accident occurs. The low-risk group's expected utility, EV^L, for this insurance arrangement is then

$$(1) \qquad EV^L = p^L\, U(W-L-\pi^L q+q) + (1-p^L)\, U(W-\pi^L q)$$

where the term $(W-L-\pi^L q+q)$ is the low-risk individual's wealth if an accident occurs and $(W-\pi^L q)$ is the low-risk individual's wealth if no accident occurs. Similarly, the high-risk group's expected utility, EV^H, for this insurance arrangement is

$$(2) \qquad EV^H = p^H\, U(W-L-\pi^H q+q) + (1-p^H)\, U(W-\pi^H q)$$

where π^H is the high-risk rate of insurance. For all indi-viduals, the maximization problem is to choose that amount coverage, q^*, that maximizes his or her expected utility of wealth over the two states of the world. First order condi-tions for low-risk individuals yield

$$(3) \qquad \frac{U'(W-L+(1-\pi^L)q)}{U'(W-\pi^L q)}\; \frac{p^L}{1-p^L} = \frac{\pi^L}{1-\pi^L}$$

Income in the no-accident state can be exchanged for income in the accident state at a fixed rate of $\pi^L/1-\pi^L$, which is the price of insurance measured in terms of income in the no-accident state. The left-hand side of (3) is the slope of the low-risk group's indifference curve (which is expressed by the marginal utilities). The price of low-risk insurance, $\pi^L/1-\pi^L$, is the slope of the budget line. Similarly, first order conditions for high-risk individuals yield

$$(4) \qquad \frac{U'(W-L+(1-\pi^H)q)}{U'(W-\pi^H q)} \frac{p^H}{1-p^H} = \frac{\pi^H}{1-\pi^H}.$$

Notice that the slope of the high-risk group's indifference curve (the left-hand side of equation (4)) differs from the slope of the low-risk group's indifference curve (the left-hand side of equation (3)) by the difference in their riskiness, $p^H \neq p^L$. This helps explain why high-risk indifference curves are flatter than low-risk indifference curves in the graphical analyses that follow.

It is assumed that insurance firms are risk neutral and are concerned only with maximizing expected profits. It is also assumed, for now, that firms possess perfect information in that they can identify low-risk and high-risk individuals. The supply of insurance for the low-risk group can be characterized by noting that insurance firms receive $\pi^L q - q$ dollars if accident occurs and $\pi^L q$ dollars if no accident occurs. Hence, expected profits, $E\phi^L$, for firms selling insurance contracts to the low-risk group are

$$(5) \qquad E\phi^L = (1-p^L) \pi^L q - p^L(1-\pi^L)q .$$

Assuming long-run competition forces profits of insurance firms to zero, equation (5) implies that

$$(6) \qquad \frac{\pi^L}{1-\pi^L} = \frac{p^L}{1-p^L} .$$

Condition (6) states that competitive firms supply low-risk insurance contracts at an actuarially fair price. Similarly, firms supply high-risk insurance contracts at an actuarially fair price,

$$(7) \qquad \frac{\pi^H}{1-\pi^H} = \frac{p^H}{1-p^H}$$

based on their expected profits, $E\phi^H$,

$$(8) \qquad E\phi^H = (1-p^H)\pi^H q - p^H(1-\pi^H)q ,$$

for selling insurance contracts to the high-risk group.

To characterize market behavior in a competitive insurance market, simply insert (6) and (7) into the low-risk and high-risk group's first order conditions, equations (3) and (4) respectively. This results in

$$(9) \qquad U'(W-L+(1-\pi^L)q) = U'(W-\pi^L q)$$

for the low-risk group and

$$(10) \qquad U'(W-L+(1-\pi^H)q) = U'(W-\pi^H q)$$

for the high-risk group. And assuming that utility is independent of the state, equations (9) and (10) imply that

$$(11) \qquad L = q .$$

Thus, low-risk and high-risk individuals will fully insure when faced with actuarially fair prices for insurance.

Outcomes in a competitive accident insurance market with perfect information are illustrated in Figure 3.1 where the horizontal axis measures wealth in the no-accident state, W_{na}, and the vertical axis measures wealth in the accident state, W_a. Assume both low-risk and high-risk individuals start with an initial endowment (W-L,W) at point E in an uninsured state. The set of contracts offered by a firm for low-risk individuals which just breaks even is given by equation (5) and is depicted in Figure 3.1 by the line EL, where $-(1-\pi^L)/\pi^L$ is the slope.[5] Similarly, the set of contracts offered by a firm for high-risk individuals which just breaks even is derived from equation (8) and is denoted by line EH. The slopes of both lines reflect the price of insurance for each risk group, $\pi^L = p^L$ for the low-risk group and $\pi^H = p^H$ for the high-risk group. Thus, line EH is flatter than line EL since $p^H > p^L$. Indifference curves for low-risk and high-risk groups are derived from equations (3) and (4) and they are placed in Figure 3.1 as U^L and U^H respectively.

Recall that a competitive insurance market with no information problems (i.e., firms are able to identify low-risk and high-risk groups) can be characterized by individuals fully insuring by purchasing actuarially fair insurance contracts. This result is illustrated graphically by noting that any point on a 45° line in Figure 3.1 represents full-insurance (complete coverage) since a point on the line equates wealth in the accident state, W_a, with wealth in the no-accident state, W_{na}. Thus market outcomes will occur at the tangency of each risk group's indifference curve to its respective contract line intersecting at the 45° line. Market equilibrium, then, results in contracts α^L and α^H purchased by low-risk and high-risk individuals respectively.

The R-S-W model now demonstrates the effects of information problems on market outcomes. Let us focus on the most common problem in accident insurance: informational asymmet-

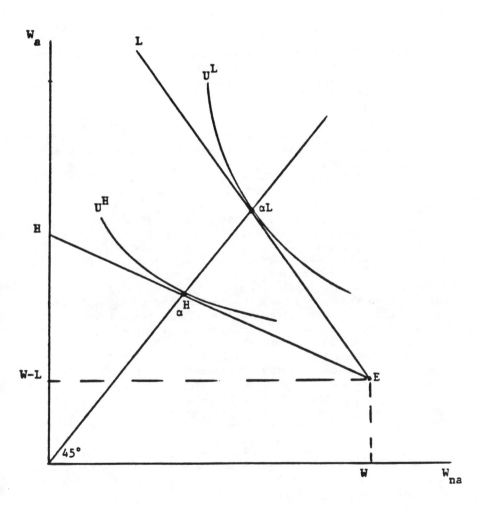

FIGURE 3.1

ries.[6] Asymmetric information in an accident insurance market exists when firms are unable to distinguish among consumers according to their probabilities of incurring accident. As a consequence, firms are unable to differentiate between low-risk and high-risk individuals so adverse selection problems may arise. And as Wilson (113) reveals, a market's resolution of adverse selection problems results in either a separating equilibrium (the offering of separate contracts to low-risk and high-risk groups) or a pooling equilibrium (the offering of a single contract to all individuals in the market). The final result depends on the proportion of low-risk and high-risk individuals in the market and an assumption made about market equilibrium.

A Wilson equilibrium is employed throughout the analyses.[7] A Wilson equilibrium involves some foresight on the part of each firm. In a Wilson equilibrium the optimal set of policies offered by each firm is determined under the assumption that any currently marketed policies which become unprofitable as a result of their new offerings will no longer be offered. Compared with the conventional Nash equilibrium assumption (employed by Rothschild and Stiglitz (93)), a Wilson equilibrium is elaborate. In a Nash equilibrium each firm is assumed to determine the set of contracts it will offer under the assumption that all other firms make no changes in their current offerings. It is clear that if a Nash equilibrium exists, it is also a Wilson equilibrium. However, the converse does not necessarily follow.

Outcomes in a competitive accident insurance market with asymmetric information are illustrated in Figure 3.2. Again, the sets of contracts offered by a firm for low-risk and high-risk groups which just break even are placed in the diagram as lines EL and EH respectively. Indifference curves are of the usual shape and are labeled U^L for the low-risk group and U^H for the high-risk group. Following the previous analysis, if firms can identify the low-risk group (the perfect information case), the contract set (α^H, α^L) represents market equilibrium. In other words, both low-risk and high-risk groups purchase full insurance on their actuarially fair contract lines. However, if the insurance market is assumed to possess an informational asymmetry in that firms are not able to differentiate between low-risk and high-risk individuals, adverse selection may result. High-risk individuals may then obtain contracts intended for low-risk individuals. For if firms were to offer contracts α^L and α^H, high-risk individuals would no longer be content with α^H, since α^L offers more wealth in both states of the world. Firms offering the contract set (α^H,α^L) would then lose money since both types of individuals purchase contract α^L. Thus the contract set (α^H,α^L) is not a Wilson equilibrium (or even a Nash equilibrium).

The potential problem of adverse selection, then, forces firms to alter their contract offerings away from the perfect

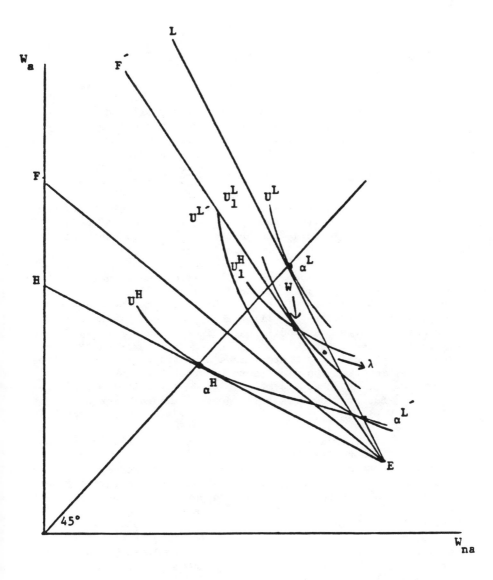

FIGURE 3.2

41

information case.   And as stated earlier, the market's resolution, the offering of separating or pooling contracts, depends
on the composition of low-risk and high-risk individuals in the
market.   Let us consider the case where line   EF in Figure 3.2
represents the market fair odds line of low-risk and high-risk
individuals in the market.   The only set of contracts that
satisfy a Wilson equilibrium is the separating set $(\alpha^H, \alpha^{L'})$.
An offer of these contracts will keep high-risk individuals at
α^H, since $\alpha^{L'}$ is on U^H. Low-risk individuals, however, are
forced to purchase $\alpha^{L'}$ where they consume less than full coverage.   To see that this separating arrangement is an equilibrium, notice that the low-risk group's indifference curve passing through point $\alpha^{L'}$, $U^{L'}$, lies to the right of the market
fair odds line, EF.   It follows that any pooling contract offered on line EF incurs losses since the low-risk group prefers
$\alpha^{L'}$ to it.   Thus, the separating contract set $(\alpha^H, \alpha^{L'})$ is a
Wilson equilibrium (and obviously also a Nash equilibrium).

Now consider the case where line EF' in Figure 3.2
represents the market fair odds line of low-risk and high-risk
individuals in the market, with more low-risk individuals than
in the case when EF was the fair odds line.   It is easily demonstrated that the Wilson separating equilibrium $(\alpha^H, \alpha^{L'})$ will
not exist.   To see this, notice that the low-risk individual's
indifference curve, $U^{L'}$, through point $\alpha^{L'}$, lies below the
market fair odds line, EF'.   There exists a pooling contract
W preferred by both low-risk and high-risk individuals to $(\alpha^H,$
$\alpha^{L'})$. Hence, $(\alpha^H, \alpha^{L'})$ is not an equilibrium since firms offering it eventually incur losses.   However, it can be shown that
W is a pooling Wilson equilibrium.   To see this notice that
low-risk and high-risk individual's indifference curves U_1^L and
U_1^H pass through point W.   Since U_1^H is flatter than U_1^L (see
equations (3) and (4)) there exists a contract λ that is preferred by low-risk individuals to contract W, so some insurance
firms can be expected to offer it and attract low-risk customers.   But as low-risk individuals leave contract W, firms
offering W will incur losses since they serve only high-risk
customers.   Eventually firms do not offer contract W so that
high-risk individuals then purchase contract λ which then
ultimately incurs losses.   The pooling contract W is a Wilson
equilibrium since firms are assumed to have the foresight to
know that the offerings of contracts such as λ eventually lead
to unprofitable outcomes and thus do not offer such contracts.

Notice that the pooling Wilson equilibrium, W, is at a
point where the low-risk group's indifference curve is tangent
to the market fair odds line, EF'.   Any other contract offered
on line EF' results in losses since the low-risk group always
prefers W.   Thus, the coverage level of a pooling contract is
determined by the low-risk group.

The R-S-W model developed in this section demonstrates the
importance of information problems on market outcomes.   Again,
to review, a market's resolution of adverse selection problems

results in either a separating equilibrium or a pooling equilibrium. The final result depends on the composition of low-risk
and high-risk individuals in the market. If a separating equilibrium exists, the low-risk group is forced to partially insure on its actuarially fair contract line, while the high-risk
group purchases full coverage at an actuarially fair price.
And if a pooling equilibrium exists, the low-risk group, in effect, subsidizes the high-risk group, since they both purchase
insurance at the same price which is greater than the low-risk
group's actuarially fair price and lower than the high-risk
group's actuarially fair price. In either case, information
problems have a direct impact on market participants. An examination of today's insurance markets, then, has to take account
of the market's inherent information problems. The following
sections consider information problems while examining accident
insurance markets.

RATE REGULATION

The effects of rate regulation on market outcomes are now
examined. Since 1945 rate regulation has aimed at setting
minimum prices, justified on the ground that competition would
lead to instability of pricing with harmful consequences for
firm solvency.[8] Although the type of regulatory control over
prices differs from state to state, a general rate setting
formula is used in most states. The pricing formula for rates
of a particular line of insurance is one which sets insurance
rates to cover losses, expenses, and a profit factor "loading"
(usually 5% of premiums) based on aggregate experience for the
industry as a whole in the particular state.[9]

Rate regulation as described above requires the prior
approval by government of insurance rate changes.[10] Approvals
are common for upward rate deviations but only under very
limited circumstances are downward deviations approved.[11] Thus
under this particular arrangement, rate regulation inhibits
price competition and we would expect to find regulated insurance rates at higher levels than their competitive counterparts. This claim is substantiated by Saba (94) who presents
empirical evidence that the behavior of insurance firms is consistent with a model of an insurance market where the regulated
rate is fixed above the competitive rate. Saba demonstrates,
for the automobile insurance market, that rate regulation results in firms operating to the left of the minimum point
of their average cost curves, a finding that suggests that
regulated automobile insurance rates are fixed above their
competitive counterparts. MacAvoy (68) also reports that rate
regulation discourages rate reductions, and further suggests
that rate regulation contributes to instability in insurance
market operations.

The above discussion suggests that a regulated insurance market may be characterized by noting that regulated insurance rates are on average higher than competitive rates, while regulated firms have less flexibility in price deviations than competitive firms.[12]   Higher regulated rates, however do not necessarily imply positive profits. Following Joskow's empirical evidence (53) supports the view that accident insurance markets possess a competitive market structure and despite cartel-like pricing, free entry tends to drive profits toward the cost of capital. Thus regulated contract offer lines in the graphs that follow are still assumed zero-profit lines. Before proceeding it must be reiterated that emphasis is on how rate regulation affects market outcomes in the context of information problems. The question of whether rate regulation provides benefits, such as securing firm solvency, is deferred to a later section.

The basic model is extended to include rate regulation by inserting π_R (where $\pi_R > \pi_C$) into the low- and high-risk group's first order conditions, which are equations (3) and (4) respectively. These insertions yield

$$(12) \qquad \frac{U'(W-L+(1-\pi_R^L)q)}{U'(W-\pi_R^L q)} = \frac{1-p^L}{p^L} \frac{\pi_R^L}{1-\pi_R^L} > 1$$

for the low-risk group, and

$$(13) \qquad \frac{U'(W-L+(1-\pi_R^L)q)}{U'(W-\pi_R^H q)} = \frac{1-p^L}{p^H} \frac{\pi_R^L}{1-\pi_R^L} > 1$$

for the high-risk group. For the low-risk group (equation (12)), it follows that $U'(W-L + (1-\pi_R^L)q)$ must be greater than $U'(W-\pi_R^L q)$. In other words, the marginal utility of wealth in the accident state must be greater than the marginal utility of wealth in the no-accident state. Thus, q must be less than L, since a decrease in the value of the wealth prospect increases the marginal utility of wealth. Only a decrease in q will equate (12) when π_R^L is the low-risk regulated rate. Similarly, for the high-risk group, only a decrease in q will equate (13) when π_R^H is the high-risk regulated rate. Hence, where price is regulated above its competitive level, individuals will not fully insure even though they are risk-averse.[13]

Rate regulation affects the supply of insurance by noting that regulated firms now offer insurance contracts to low-risk and high-risk groups at the regulated rates, π_R^L and π_R^H respectively. Thus expected profits, $E\phi_R^L$, for regulated firms selling insurance contracts to the low-risk group are

$$(14) \qquad E\phi_R^L = (1-p^L)\pi_R^L q - p^L(1-\pi_R^2)q$$

and expected profits, $E\phi_R^H$, for regulated firms selling insurance contracts to the high-risk group are

$$(15) \qquad E\phi_R^H = (1-p^H)\ \pi_R^H q\ -\ p^H(1-\pi_R^H)q.$$

Recall that the slopes of the non-regulated contract lines in Figure 3.1 are $1-\pi^L/\pi^L$ for the low-risk group and $1-\pi^H/\pi^H$ for the high-risk group. Since regulation sets $\pi_R^L > \pi^L$ and $\pi_R^H > \pi^H$, the slopes of the regulated contract offerings are flatter than their competitive counterparts. This of course is consistent with underinsuring.

Outcomes in an accident insurance market with rate regulation are illustrated in Figure 3.3. The market is divided into two risk groups, low-risk and high-risk, with corresponding actuarially fair (non-regulated) contract lines EL and EH. Recall, the market's resolution to firms' inabilities to identify low-risk individuals results in either a separating equilibrium $(\alpha^H, \alpha^{L'})$ or a pooling equilibrium, W, depending on the composition of low-and high-risk individuals in the market. Let us begin with the pooling equilibrium, W, assuming a low proportion of high-risk individuals represented by the market fair odds line EF. Thus, line EF lies to the right of the low-risk group's indifference curve, U^L passing through point $U^{L'}$. In this non-regulated environment, firms offer the competitive pooling contract W to both low-and high-risk individuals on their zero-profit (market fair odds) line EF. Rate regulation results in the market setting a price for a pooling contract that is greater than the price charged for the competitive pooling W contract. Thus, the regulated contract offer line must lie to the left of the non-regulated offer line (market fair odds line) EF. Notice that the regulated offer line is still a zero-profit line since free entry drives profits to zero.[14]

There are two possible effects of rate regulation on market outcomes. First, the regulated pooled contract price, π_R^P, might be greater than the competitive pooled price, π_C^P, such that the regulated market offers the regulated contract line EF_R. In this case the regulated pooling contract W_R, offering less coverage than W, is offered. This is because the low-risk group determines the coverage level of a pooling contract, and the low-risk group decreases coverage in response to a price increase. Thus, in this first case, rate regulation forces both risk groups to purchase less coverage at a higher price and both are obviously made worse off. However, there exists a second possible outcome of rate regulation. Consider a regulated pooled contract π_R^{P*} such that the regulated pooled contract line is line EF_R^*. In this case, rate regulation may eliminate any possibility of a pooling equilibrium. To see this, notice that the regulated offer line EF_R^* lies to the left

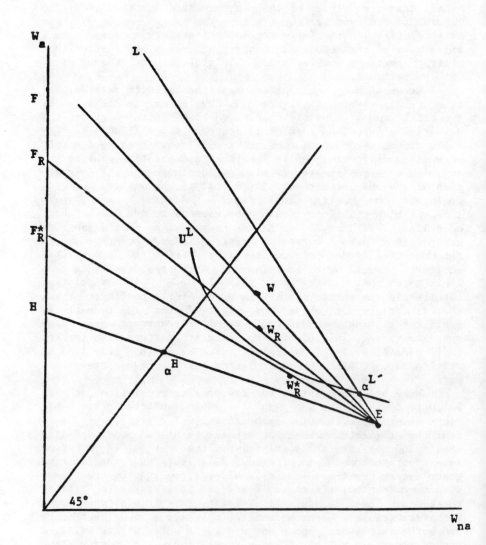

FIGURE 3.3

46

of the low-risk group's indifference curve, U^L. Thus, firms eventually offer pooling contract W_R^* (determined by maximizing the low-risk group's benefits). However, if firms are allowed to offer the separating contract set $(\alpha^H, \alpha^{L'})$, the pooling contract W_R^* is not an equilibrium since the low-risk group prefers contract $\alpha^{L'}$ to it. In this situation then, rate regulation eliminates the existence of a pooling contract. Even if firms are not permitted to offer the contract set $(\alpha^H, \alpha^{L'})$, the offering of the pooling W_R^* contract may be short-lived. Firms anticipating potential expected profits petition the regulatory board until the contract set $(\alpha^H, \alpha^{L'})$ is permitted to be offered. If its offering is denied, the pooling W_R^* contract becomes the regulated market's 'artificial' equilibrium. However, it is likely that the separating set will be approved since its policies are based on each risk group's expected costs.

Imposing rate regulation on pooling insurance policies may affect market outcomes in several ways. In the simplest case, regulated pooling contract policies induce consumers to decrease the amount of coverage desired and both risk groups are made worse off (moving from W to W_R in Figure 3.3). By raising price, rate regulation may eliminate a pooling contract from being an equilibrium, if a separating contract offering is permitted. The effects of rate regulation for this particular case are ambiguous. Using a Pareto-welfare criterion, rate regulation makes society worse off since both low-risk and high-risk groups are made worse off, going from W to W_R^* or from W to $(\alpha^H, \alpha^{L'})$. However, a separating contract might be preferred to a pooling contract on efficiency grounds since the high-risk group now pays a price for insurance that is associated with that group's expected costs, while the low-risk group also pays an actuarially fair price for insurance even though it is forced to partially insure.

Figure 3.4 illustrates the effects of rate regulation on market outcomes from an initial separating equilibrium. The market fair odds line EF is placed to the left of the low-risk group's indifference curve, U^L, passing through point $\alpha^{L'}$ so that market equilibrium requires that firms offer the non-regulated separating set of contracts $(\alpha^H, \alpha^{L'})$. Rate regulation results in the market setting prices π_R^L and π_R^H for corresponding low-risk and high-risk groups that are greater than their competitive counterparts, π^L and π^H. Thus the regulated contract offer lines for low- and high-risk groups must lie to the left of the non-regulated offer lines, EL and EH. There are two possible effects of rate regulation on market outcomes. First, the regulated prices are π_R^L and π_R^H such that the market offers the regulated contract lines E_R^L and E_R^H to low- and high-risk groups respectively. In this case, the regulated separating equilibrium $(\alpha_R^H, \alpha_R^{L'})$ exists, since U_2^L lies to the right of the market fair odds line EF. This particular rate regulation, then, makes both low- and high-risk groups worse-off by forcing the low-risk group to purchase less insurance at a higher price (going from α^L to $\alpha_R^{L'}$) and forcing the high-risk also to purchase less insurance at a higher price (going from α^H to α_R^H).

The second possible outcome of rate regulation is more interesting and is illustrated in Figure 3.5 below. Let us assume that rate regulation results in the market setting prices π_R^{L*} and π_R^{H*} such that the regulated offer lines to low- and high-risk groups are E_R^{L*} and E_R^{H*} respectively. In this case, rate regulation may eliminate any possibility of a separating equilibrium. To see this, notice that the separating contracts offered (α_R^{H*}, α_R^{L*}) on contract lines E_R^{L*} and E_R^{H*} results in the low-risk group's indifference curve, U_3^L, which lies to the left of the market fair odds line EF. Thus, if firms are permitted to pool individuals, any firm offering (α_R^{H*}, α_R^{L*}) incurs losses since the low-risk group prefers a pooling W contract to it. In this situation, rate regulation eliminates the existence of a separating equilibrium. And even if firms are not initially permitted to offer the pooling W contract, firms anticipating potential profits will petition the regulatory board until the W pooling contract is allowed to be offered. In this particular case, rate regulation may prevent a separating equilibrium. The high-risk group is made better off (going from α^H to W) and the low-risk group is made worse off (going from $\alpha^{L'}$ to W). It is interesting to note that the low-risk group is forced to purchase more insurance at a higher price, while the high-risk group is forced to purchase less insurance at a lower price.

Thus findings suggest that rate regulation may affect market outcomes in more profound ways than just increased prices and low desired coverage levels. In some situations rate regulation might alter a market's policy offerings. Regulation may inadvertantly force firms to switch from offering pooling contracts to offering separating contracts, or vice versa, depending on the riskiness composition of individuals in the market. The question of whether regulation can aid in the market's process of dealing with information problems is addressed later.

The implications of price flexibility on insurance market outcomes are now examined. Recall from an earlier discussion that regulated firms have less flexibility in price deviations than competitive firms. These differences in price flexibility are attributed to the fact that rate regulation employs a prior approval system while a more flexible (competitive) rate setting environment employs a file and use system. Under prior approval, any insurance rate change requires the prior approval by government (the insurance commission). And as previously stated, approvals are common for upward rate deviations but only under very limited circumstances are downward deviations approved. The file and use system provides that rates become effective immediately upon filing by an insurance firm and that

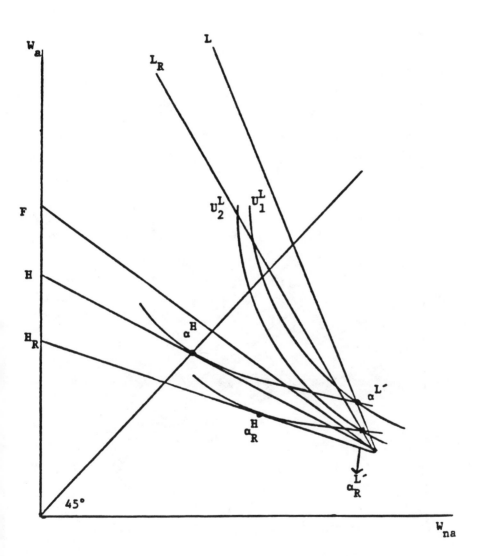

FIGURE 3.4

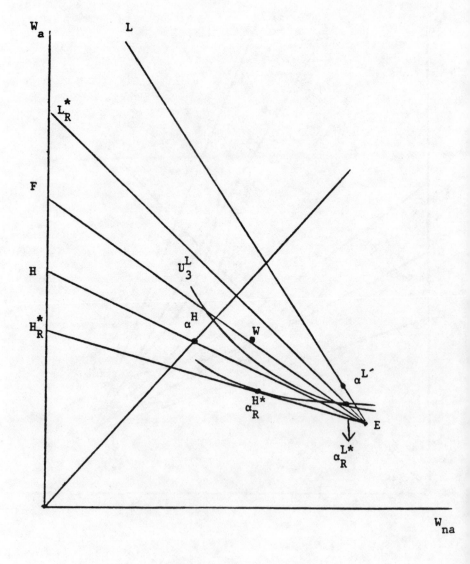

FIGURE 3.5

the Commissioner could subsequently disapprove any rate found to be excessive or unreasonable.[15] No approval prior to use is required.

The effects of a prior approval (inflexible) rate system on insurance market outcomes are illustrated in Figure 3.6. Let us begin by placing in the diagram the low- and high-risk actuarially fair contract lines EL and EH, and the market fair odds line EF. Also allow for the possibility that market conditions can change over time. Consider the possibility that the riskiness of each risk group (low and high) changes over time. For example, assume that a neighborhood deteriorates over time. Deterioration might result in traffic congestion, which may increase the probability of automobile accidents, or in unkept buildings of the fire hazard variety, resulting in an increase in the probability of fire-related accidents. Deterioration, then, increases a group's riskiness. On the other hand, the restoration of neighborhoods (e.g., inner cities) may reduce a group's riskiness. Improvements in neighborhoods may result in better driving conditions and/or safer fire-preventive buildings. Specifically changes in riskiness are depicted by letting the low-risk group fair odds line vary between EL_1 and EL_2 and the high-risk group's fair odds line vary between EH_1 and EH_2. For simplicity of exposition assume that each risk group's riskiness changes in the same proportion and that the change is in the same direction. For example, when EH changes to EH_1, EL changes to EL_1 and the distance between EH and EH_1 is equal to the distance between EL and EL_1. And since the market fair odds line consists of the low- and high-risk groups, it also varies, between EF_1 and EF_2. With the diagram now able to illustrate changing market conditions, the examination of prior approval begins.

Let us begin from an initial pooling equilibrium so that the pooling contract W on the market fair odds line EF is offered.[16] Suppose that the riskiness of the entire group increases due to changing market conditions. Graphically, this change is represented by a movement from line EF to line EF_1 (also keep in mind that lines EL_1 and EH_1 now exist). It is important to note that, since riskiness has changed, the line EF_1 now becomes the market fair odds line and that the slopes for both risk groups' indifference curves are affected by this change, since their p's are in equations (3) and (4). Thus, in light of these events, firms petition the regulatory board for a rate increase so that the pooling contract W_1 can be offered.[17] If the petition is granted, firms offer the pooling contract W_1 on the zero-profit line, EF_1. However, since firms need prior approval before they can offer policy W , they continue to offer W_1 until the rate increase is approved. Thus, firms incur short-run losses selling contract W under this arrangement.[18]

Suppose market conditions change such that the pooled group's riskiness, represented by the market fair odds line EF,

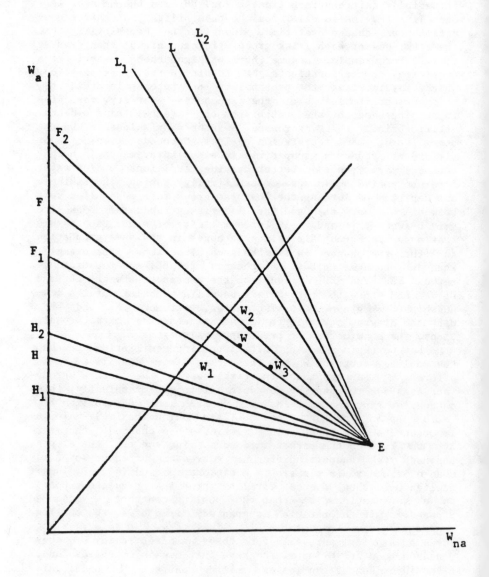

FIGURE 3.6

has decreased so that line EF_2 becomes the market fair odds line. Firms then petition the regulatory board for a rate decrease so that they can offer the pooling contract W_2. Again, the position of W_2 on line EF_2 is determined by maximizing the low-risk group's benefits whose actuarially fair contract line is now EL_2. However, suppose the request for a rate decrease is denied (a likely occurrence under the prior approval system) so that firms are unable to offer contract W_2. Thus firms continue offering the contract represented by line EF. But to the low-risk group (whose actuarially fair contract line is EL_2) the insurance rate reflected by line EF represents a price increase since their risk has been lowered. Hence, the low-risk group reduces coverage and chooses a pooling contract W_3 which lies to the right of the original pooling contract, W, since their indifference curves are now steeper. In this case, because the request for a rate decrease was denied, both risk groups are forced to purchase less insurance by purchasing contract W_3. Notice that line EF is still a zero-profit line, since free entry and non-price competition drives profits towards zero. The prior approval system, then, results in firms realizing short-term losses for rate increases, and firms being forced to offer low-coverage pooling contracts and engage in unnecessary non-price competition as a consequence of a rate change denial.

The inflexibility of price deviations under prior approval also affects market outcomes in an indirect, though obvious, way. Recognizing that in a free market price disseminates information about changing market conditions, it is possible that the prior approval system impairs firms' abilities to detect (and of course respond to) changing market conditions. In terms of our diagram (Figure 3.6), not only do prior approval firms have difficulty in responding to changes in riskiness (offering pooling contracts that are closely associated with the expected costs of the pooled risk group) but they may be slow to detect a change in consumer riskiness since that information is no longer being reflected in price reductions by other firms (since prices are rigid downward). For example, firms may be unaware that the market fair odds line is shifting from EF to EF_1, and continue offering contract W. Thus, not until a substantial amount of risk-related information is collected and subsequent losses are incurred, do firms petition the regulatory board for a rate increase. Similarly, if the market fair odds line shifts to EF_2, firms will be slow in detecting this change and consequently earn short-term profits. The prior approval system then in inhibiting detection and responses to changing market conditions may contribute to instability in insurance market operations. Indeed, our findings suggest that insurance operations under prior approval (with large fluctuations in profits and losses) are less stable than a competitive market's insurance operations (where firms have more flexibility in reacting to changing market conditions).

MINIMUM INSURANCE COVERAGE REQUIREMENTS

A government interference on the buyer side, minimum insurance coverage requirements, is now examined. Minimum coverage requirements are particularly common in automobile insurance. Most states now require individuals to purchase a minimum of \$10,000/\$20,000 liability coverage. Figure 3.7 illustrates the effects of minimum coverage requirements on market outcomes from an initial separating equilibrium. The market fair odds line EF is placed to the left of the low-risk group's indifference curve U^L passing through point $\alpha^{L'}$ so that market equilibrium requires that firms offer the separating contract set $(\alpha^H, \alpha^{L'})$. Consider the case where a minimum coverage restriction, q^*, is imposed on all individuals in the market. Such a restriction is represented by the horizontal line q^*m in the diagram. The restriction dictates that all individuals must purchase insurance coverage on or above the line q^*m. High-risk individuals are not affected by the minimum coverage imposition. However, the restriction is binding for low-risk individuals. Firms now are forced to offer contract $\alpha^{L''}$ to the low-risk group. But the set of contracts $(\alpha^H, \alpha^{L''})$ is not an equilibrium because the high-risk group now can be made better off by purchasing $\alpha^{L''}$. Firms would then incur losses, since any point on line EL represents zero profits for firms before high-risk individuals purchased low-risk contracts. Thus, $(\alpha^H, \alpha^{L''})$ is not offered. However, if firms charge a price greater than the actuarially fair price to low-risk individual's a possible set of contracts may exist. In the diagram, the higher-priced low-risk contract line EL' is such a line. Firms can offer contract $\alpha^{L'''}$ to the low-risk group and keep the high-risk group satisfied with purchasing contract α^H since α^H and $\alpha^{L'''}$ both lie on the high-risk group's indifference curve U^H. Also notice that $\alpha^{L'''}$ satisfies the minimum coverage restriction since it lies on q^*m. Thus, the contract set $(\alpha^H, \alpha^{L'''})$ is a workable separating set that satisfies the coverage requirements. And line EL' eventually is a zero-profit line since free entry and non-price competition drives profits towards zero. However, the contract set $(\alpha^H, \alpha^{L'''})$ is not an equilibrium set.[19] To see this notice that the low-risk group's indifference curve, U^L_1, passing through point $\alpha^{L'''}$ lies to the left of the market fair odds line EF. There exists, then, a pooling contract W, that when offered, is preferred by both low-risk and high-risk groups. Hence, the set $(\alpha^H, \alpha^{L'''})$ is not an equilibrium and firms now offer the pooling contract W which is an equilibrium.

The above analysis suggests that if minimum coverage requirements are binding, firms may be forced to switch from offering separating contracts to offering pooling contracts. Coverage restrictions, then, may directly affect a way firms deal with information problems since separating contracts are a firm's way of alleviating adverse selection problems by

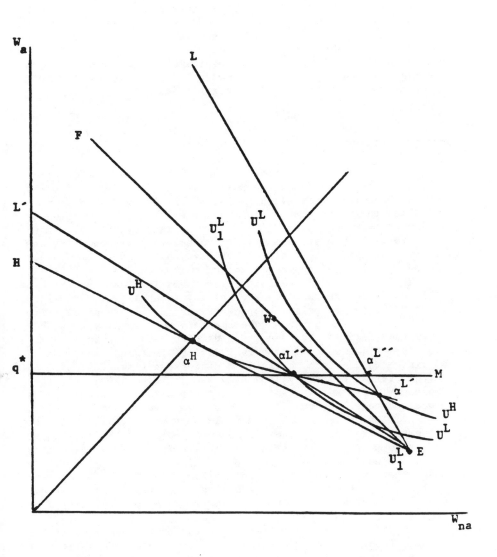

FIGURE 3.7

55

inducing individuals to self-select.   It is   then important to assess the performance of minimum coverage requirements   in the context of information problems.[20]

The   altered policy offerings that   minimum   coverage requirements impose   on market outcomes do not   necessarily imply that minimum coverage restrictions cannot   perform   a useful function.   Individuals choosing   not to purchase insurance may not be in a financial position to pay off   liabilities incurred during   accident.   And since   some accidents   impose costs   on others (e.g., two-car automobile accidents),   coverage requirements   might   reduce liability   costs and   thus   minimize costs imposed on outside   parties (in   our case,   the   innocent automobile owner).   Whether these   requirements are necessary is a question we   must leave to   others who   seek to weigh   the full benefits and costs of insurance regulation.

CONSUMER MISINFORMATION

In the   previous sections,   insurance   market   information problems were   focused on the seller side.   For example, firms were assumed to possess information about   individual riskiness which led to several market related problems.   This section is concerned with incomplete information on the buyer side.   More specifically,   the situation where consumers know   their probabilities of incurring accident but have poor   information about the availability of insurance policies is examined.

The   problems of   consumer misinformation that   prevail in accident insurance   markets are   nicely pointed   out   by Joskow (53): "Comparative price shopping is very difficult since price differences for comparable coverages are not   readily available in printed form and because it is difficult to   obtain information from friends and neighbors...Asking him about insurance is of little value since he   is in a differenct risk   class, lives in a different community, and drives a different kind   of car." Two empirical studies also support the position   that consumers have imperfect   information in   obtaining   insurance   policies. Cummins et al (23) finds   in a field survey of   individuals who purchase   automobile and/or   homeowners coverage that   few compare the   policy terms   from different companies   before making their purchase decision.   And a   field survey of homeowners by Kunreuther et   al (63)   reveals similar   behavior.[21]   Particularly,   the   study   reveals   that most   homeowners   are either unaware of terms   in their   policies or have   misinformation on such data as premiums and deductibles.[22]

State regulatory commissions in the past have   done little to alleviate this consumer information problem.   Only recently have some state commissions begun to deal with the   problems of information availability.   States which   are turning towards a competitive   rating system   (e.g., Virginia)   are   beginning to provide information in the form of published guides, on price differences among firms.

The effects of consumer misinformation on market outcomes are two-fold. First, consumer misinformation may upset the equilibrium process which determines the market's policy offerings (i.e., separating and pooling contracts). For example, a consumer not knowing if a certain separating contract is available might purchase a lower coverage contract or a pooling contract. Thus even though the market's composition of riskiness dictates a separating contract arrangement, pooling contracts may survive. Second, consumer misinformation may result in consumers purchasing policies at prices that are greater than the actuarially fair price.

The first case, how consumer misinformation alters the market's policy offerings, is illustrated in Figure 3.8 below. The market fair odds line EF is placed to the left of the low-risk group's indifference curve U^L passing through point $\alpha^{L'}$ so that a separating equilibrium exists. Consumers with correct information about the availability of policies purchase the separating set $(\alpha^H, \alpha^{L'})$. Consumer misinformation, however, may affect a firm's policy offering strategies. To see this notice that the separating set $(\alpha^H, \alpha^{L'})$ is no longer a unique equilibrium since its existence depends on the assumption that consumers have perfect information concerning the availability of insurance policy offerings. Thus firms, aware that some consumers are unaware of the separating offering $(\alpha^H, \alpha^{L'})$, have incentive to vary the separating contract coverage levels, or even to offer pooling contracts. These possible contract offerings are illustrated in Figure 3.8. Let us begin with firms offering the separating contract set $(\alpha^H, \alpha^{L'})$ to all individuals in the market. Firms aware that some consumers may be misinformed about the availability of $(\alpha^H, \alpha^{L'})$ may attempt to vary the coverage levels of the separating contracts. For example, firms might reduce the low-risks group's coverage level and offer a contract $\alpha_1^{L'}$ to them. This offering is a viable one since misinformed low-risk individuals purchase it, while high-risk individuals continue to purchase α^H (since they prefer α^H to $\alpha^{L'}$). Thus, the offering of $\alpha^{L'}$ is a likely case. However, firms offering low-risk individuals higher coverage, such as contract $\alpha^{L'}$, are unlikely since it is preferred by all individuals (misinformed and informed high and low risk). Also firms may offer lower-coverage high-risk policies, such as α_1^H, since it is purchased only by misinformed high-risk individuals. Finally, the possibility that firms offer a pooling W contract is unlikely. As Figure 3.8 depicts, misinformed low-risk individuals purchase W but informed low-risk individuals do not since they prefer $\alpha^{L'}$ to it. And since all high-risk individuals prefer W to α^H, the pooling W contract incurs losses and is not offered.

Figure 3.8 also illustrates the effects of consumer misinformation from an initial pooling equilibrium. Let line EF'

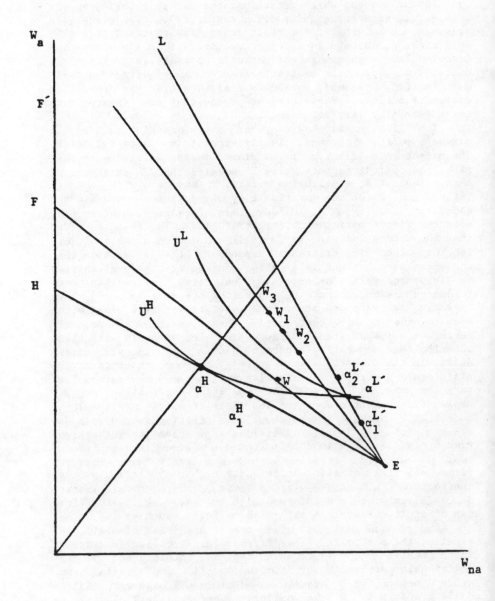

FIGURE 3.8

represent the market fair odds line so that the pooling contract W_1 is an equilibrium. Consumer misinformation may affect the market in the following way. Firms may offer lower coverage pooled policies, such as W_2 or higher-coverage pooled policies such as W_3. If the low-coverage W_2 policy is offered, misinformed low- and high-risk individuals purchase it, while informed low- and high-risk individuals prefer W_1 to it. Thus the existence of both W_1 and W_2 contracts depends on the composition of misinformed low-and high-risk individuals in the market. For example, there exists the possibility that if there are more misinformed low-risk individuals than there are misinformed high-risk individuals, contract W_2 is feasible while any firm offering contract W_1 incurs losses since a higher proportion of high-risk individuals purchase it. Also, the offering of the high-coverage W_3 policy is unlikely. To see this, recall that the position of a pooling contract is determined by the tangency of the low-risk group's indifference curve to the market fair odds line (in other words, firms maximize low-risk benefits). Thus, informed low-risk individuals prefer contract W_1 to any other contract offering on line EF´. Contract W_3, then, is purchased by misinformed low-and high-risk individuals and also by the informed high-risk individuals, but is not purchased by informed low-risk individuals. It follows that any firms offering contract W_3 incur losses since there is a disproportionate amount of high-risk individuals.

Finally, firms may offer separating contracts in response to consumer misinformation problems. For example, the separating set (α^H, $\alpha^{L´}$) may be feasible. This may work because informed low-risk and high-risk individuals continue purchasing W_1, while misinformed individuals self-select into the separating contracts. Thus, with misinformed consumers it is possible that a separating and pooled contract can co-exist. Notice that if the composition of the informed low-risk and high-risk individuals differs from the composition of all low-risk and high-risk individuals in the market (this includes, informed and misinformed) then the market fair odds line for the informed individuals who continue to purchase a pooling contract, changes. The market fair odds line EF´ either rotates upward or downward depending on the market composition. Hence, consumer misinformation may result not only in the market offering separating and pooling contracts side by side, but also in changes in the riskiness composition of pooling contracts.

The above examinations suggest that consumer misinformation problems have a significant impact on a market's policy offerings when examined in a context of informational asymmetries. Indeed, consumer misinformation permits multiple equilibria contract offerings in the marketplace. However, a bias exists in that firms will lower policy coverage levels but not raise them in response to consumer misinformation. And the bias holds for both pooling and separating contracts. Also if

the market initially offers separating contracts, firms cannot
offer pooling contracts in response to consumer misinformation.
However, if the market initially offers pooling contracts,
responding to consumer misinformation, the market offers both
separating and pooling contracts. These findings suggest,
then, that it is important to assess the effects of consumer
misinformation in the context of information problems (i.e.,
informational asymmetries).

The second case, the possibility that consumer misinformation results in firms offering higher priced policies, is
illustrated in Figure 3.9 below. The market fair odds line is
EF so that the initial pooling contract W is offered. If
consumers have complete information about the availability
(prices) of insurance policies, the pooling contract W is an
equilibrium offering. Consumer misinformation, however, makes
it possible for firms to offer higher priced contracts such as
W_1 (reflected by the slope of contract line EF´) and expect
misinformed low-risk and high-risk individuals to purchase it.
The existence of contract W_1 depends on the composition of misinformed low-risk and high-risk individuals. For example, if
there are more misinformed low-risk than high-risk individuals,
contract W is a workable contract. In this case, the offering
of W_1 precludes the offering of W since firms offering W
now serve a disproportionate amount of high-risk individuals
and consequently incur losses. However, W_1 may not exist, if
there is a disproportionate amount of misinformed high-risk individuals (although contract W_1 can accommodate more high-risk
individuals than contract W_1 since contract W's price is greater). Notice that line EF´, a zero profit line because of free
entry, continues to reflect a price greater than is actuarially
fair. Competition does not drive the price towards the actuarially fair price since there is always a firm that can sell contract W_1 to a misinformed individual.

Let us assume the market fair odds line in Figure 3.9
is line EF_1 so that an initial separating equilibrium exists.
Complete consumer information, then, results in the offering of
the contract set (α^H, $\alpha^{L´}$). Consumer misinformation produces
two possible contract offerings. First, firms may offer higher-
priced contract lines EL´ and EH´ to misinformed low- and high-
risk individuals so that the separating contract (α^H_1, $\alpha^{L´}_1$) is
purchased. The separating contract is workable because mis-
informed individuals self-select into it, while informed individuals continue to purchase (α^H, $\alpha^{L´}$). Second, firms have the
option of offering the separating contract (α^H, $\alpha^{L´}_2$). Under this
arrangement misinformed low-risk individuals self-select into
purchasing contract $\alpha^{L´}_2$, while high-risk individuals are not
affected and continue to purchase contract α^H.

The examinations of this section imply that firms can take
advantage of consumer misinformation by altering coverage
levels, the types of policies offered (pooling and separating)
and ultimately the price charged for insurance coverage. And

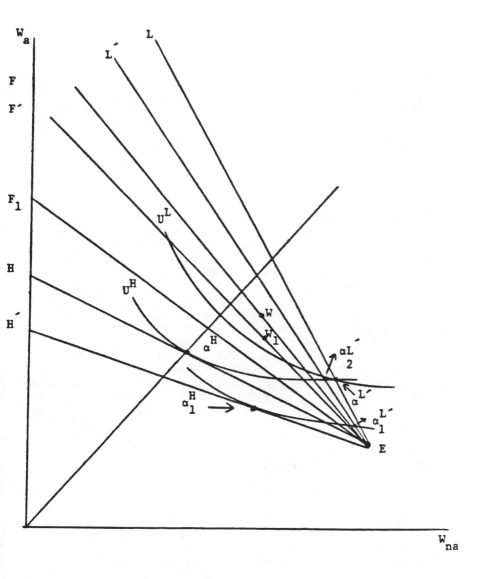

FIGURE 3.9

associated with the multiple contract offerings are lower coverage levels and higher priced policies. However, this does not imply that consumers are behaving sub-optimally in purchasing these policies. Misinformed individuals purchase contracts based on maximizing behavior. In other words, the contracts purchased represent the optimal search outcome for misinformed individuals, who cease search efforts when the marginal cost of search equals the marginal benefit gained by the additional information obtained. The problem of consumer misinformation lies not with consumer behavior but with the insurance process itself. Comparison policy shopping is difficult since the insurance process produces a product that is determined by each customer. That is, it is a customer's riskiness, based on certain risk characteristics (e.g., age, sex, type of car, and neighborhood) that determines the coverage level and expected cost for an insurance policy. And since most customers differ in riskiness, it is difficult to shop for policies.

The above discussion suggests that firms, aware of the potential advantages of consumer misinformation, may have incentive to limit the amount of information on policy availability in the marketplace. Indeed, in both regulated and competitive market settings, the problems of consumer misinformation prevail. However the existence of free entry in both market settings allows some incentives for the provision of information on policy available (e.g., new entrants will inform the market of the availability of better policies) but it may not be enough to overcome consumer misinformation. What is needed, then, is a government information service to provide the necessary information for comparison policy shopping. Where information search is costly for each individual, information gathering by the government may be virtually costless on a per person basis. Requiring all insurance firms to submit their policies with their corresponding coverage levels and prices, for each risk class and territory to state commissions (most commissions already require this) and to publish these findings, can be accomplished in an efficient low cost manner. Further, a yardstick to measure policies by should be developed to facilitate comparison.[22]

REAL WORLD INSURANCE POLICIES

To relate this study's findings to real world observations is difficult. The analyses employ an insurance market model (the R-S-W model) that is based on simplifying assumptions such as the existence of only two risk groups which possess the same initial wealth and face the same loss if accident occurs. Assumptions, however, are necessary to keep the model simple and tractable so that we may examine clearly how information problems and government interventions may affect market outcomes. Hopefully the model's findings can give us some insight into the workings of an informationally plagued and regulated insurance market. Thus, comparisons to real world markets (i.e., the property-liability insurance industry) are made but with reservations.

Examinations of the R-S-W model suggest that insurance firms, when faced with adverse selection problems, offer a menu of policies that induce customers to self-select. Low-risk individuals can signal their quality to firms by their willingness to purchase an inexpensive low coverage contract, while high-risk individuals signal their high riskiness by purchasing expensive high coverage contracts. And if this separating equilibrium does not exist, firms are forced to pool low- and high-risk groups and offer a pooling contract. That is the essence of the R-S-W model. The offering of separating and pooling contracts to deal with adverse selection problems. And as the analyses suggest, insurance regulation and consumer misinformation problems may alter the way firms deal with adverse selection. To explain real world observations in terms of these analyses, then, must require a relationship between the separating and pooling contract offerings of the R-S-W model and the current policy offerings in the property-liability insurance industry.

A cursory look into the property-liability insurance industry reveals that insurance firms offer a menu of deductible insurance policies. A deductible insurance policy requires the insured to pay for the first 'X' dollars of coverage while the insurer pays for the remaining dollars of coverage. For example, in automobile insurance a $100 deductible insurance policy for collision requires the insured pay for the first $100 of automobile damage while the insurer covers any remaining dollar claim in excess of $100. In effect, varying deductible levels of an insurance policy represents changing coverage levels for the insured. And it is observed that there is an inverse relationship between the level of deduction and the insurance rate of a particular policy. That is, a low deductible policy may be purchased at a high price for insurance, while a high deductible policy may be purchased at a lower price for the same insurance coverage. It appears that the offering of deductible insurance policies is an insurance firm's way of inducing customers to self-select into their appropriate risk groups.

Figure 3.10 helps illustrate the similarity between a separating contract generated by the R-S-W model and a deductible insurance policy offered for automobile insurance. The horizontal axis measures the amount of insurance coverage q, and the vertical axis measures the cost of insurance coverage, c. Thus, the diagram depicts insurance policies at specified coverage and cost levels. It can be illustrated how the R-S-W separating contract set (α^H, $\alpha^{L^\prime}$), first presented in Figure 3.2, can be converted into a deductible policy offering. Let lines OC_L and OC_H represent a firm's cost lines for low-risk and high-risk groups respectively. The slope of each cost line represents the cost per unit of coverage so that the high-risk cost line OC_H is steeper than the low-risk cost line OC_L since the high-risk group is more costly to serve than the low-risk group. Assuming a competitive market, the cost lines OC_L and OC_H are considered to be price lines similar to lines EL and EH in Figure 3.2. Allowing $5000 to represent the full coverage level, the separating contract set $(\alpha^H, \alpha^{L\prime})$ easily is placed in the diagram. The high-risk group is offered a full coverage ($5000) contract α^H on its cost line, OC^H, and the low-risk group is offered a partial coverage ($4000) contract $\alpha^{L\prime}$ on its cost line, OC_L. Thus the high-risk group purchases an expensive full coverage policy while the low-risk group purchases an inexpensive partial coverage policy.

The above separating arrangement can be converted into a deductible arrangement if a firm's average costs are considered. For example, let the rate of high-risk insurance coverage be set at ten cents per dollar of coverage so that the slopes of lines OC_H and OC_L are .10 and .07 respectively. It follows that at $5000 coverage, the average cost of servicing the high-risk group is $500/5000 or ten cents, while the average cost of servicing the low-risk group at $4000 coverage is $280/4000 or seven cents. To convert the low-risk $4000 partial coverage policy into a deductible low-risk policy, the firm's average cost per policy must be kept constant. For example, suppose a firm considers offering a $100 deductible low-risk policy for the same $5000 coverage that the high-risk group purchases at α^H. Let line AC_L^* in Figure 3.10 represent a $100 deductible policy offering. Notice that line AC_L^* has a $100 positive in-tercept so that a low-risk individual pays for the first $100 of coverage. Graphically, the average cost of the $100 deductible policy at a $5000 coverage level is derived by computing the slope of a line drawn from the origin to the point on line AC_L^* that corresponds to $5000 coverage. Line OC is such a line so that the average cost of the $100 deductible policy is equal to the average cost of the low-cost partial policy $\alpha^{L\prime}$ which also lies on line OC_2. Thus the low-risk $100 deductible policy α^{L*} on line AC^* carries the same average cost to a firm as the partial coverage $\alpha^{L\prime}$ low-risk insurance policy. Notice, however, that the price per unit of coverage (the marginal cost for the low-risk deductible policy) is lower than the insurance rate associated with the low-risk partial coverage policy. In summation, higher deductibles lead to higher average costs of coverage. Thus, deductibles are a way of changing different costs of coverage.

Tables 3.1 through 3.4 help illustrate the type of deductible insurance policies offered for automobile insurance. Table 3.1 presents the Aetna Casualty and Surety Company's semi-annual base automobile premiums for physical damage in New Jersey. The Table is a sample of the different deductible comprehensive and collision policies offered by Aetna to all auto-

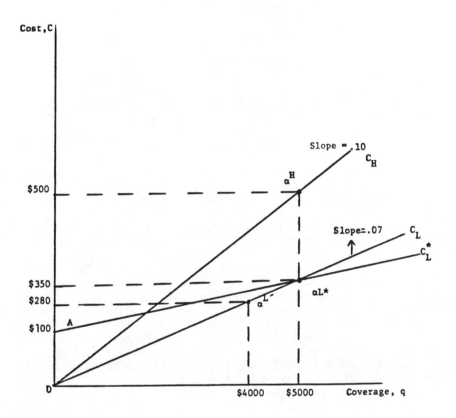

FIGURE 3.10

mobile drivers who reside in the 40 geographic regions (called
territories) in New Jersey.   Specifically, Table 3.1 presents
the semi-annual base premiums charged to customers living in
territory 1.   The headings, Age Group and Symbol Group, refer
to the age of the insured's car and the cost of the insured's
car, respectively. For example, a person living in territory 1
driving a 1982 Mercedes-Benz would be classified by the Aetna
Company in age group 1 and symbol group 7. Thus if that person
desires $100 deductible comprehensive coverage his base semi-
annual premium is $100.   Similarly, a person owning a 1968
Chevrolet Impala would be classified in age group 6 and symbol
group 1 and if he also desires $100 deductible comprehensive he
pays a semi-annual premium of $13. As the table reveals, Aetna
offers low deductible and high deductible policies (i.e., no
deductible and $100 deductible for comprehensive and $100 deductible and $200 deductible for collision). Similarly, Tables
3.2 and 3.3 present the policies offered by the Travelers Insurance company and the Prudential Property and Casualty Insurance company, and Table 3.4 presents the policies suggested by
the Insurance Services Office (ISO), a trade organization for
small insurance companies. Thus, Tables 3.1 thru 3.3 display
samples of the types of policies offered by large insurance
firms, while Table 3.4 displays the types of policies the ISO
suggests that small firms offer in the marketplace.

A comparison of the tables reveals the heterogeneous nature of policy offerings for automobile insurance. That is, the
level of deductible policies differ across firms even though
they are servicing the same market. For example, for comprehensive coverage, Aetna (Table 3.1) offers full coverage and
$100 deductible, Travelers (Table 3.2) offers full coverage and
$50 deductible, and both Prudential (Table 3.3) and ISO (Table
3.4) offer $50 and $100 deductible. For collision coverage,
Aetna offers $100 and $200 deductible, Travelers offers $100
and $250 deductible and Prudential and ISO both offer $200
deductible. And although it is difficult to compare prices
(premiums charged) since the symbol group between firms may
differ, it is observed that even though these firms are in the
same market (New Jersey) their prices often differ. Aetna and
Travelers do offer the same semi-annual premium for symbols 3
thru 8 for the $100 deductible collision.

The presence of a heterogeneous mix of deductible
insurance policies in the automobile insurance market is consistent with market outcomes in the R-S-W model. It appears
that firms offer deductible insurance policies (i.e., low
deductible high-cost policies and high deductible low-cost
policies) to deal with adverse selection problems. And since
the deductible policy offerings may differ from firm to firm,
the menu of policy offerings for automobile insurance closely
resembles market outcomes generated by an insurance market
where there are consumer misinformation problems. Indeed,
as demonstrated, consumer misinformation permits multiple

equilibria contract offerings in the marketplace. Insurance firms may take advantage of consumer misinformation by altering coverage levels, the type of policies offered, and the price charged for insurance coverage.

Although observations in the automobile insurance market (Tables 3.1 thru 3.4) are consistent with the market outcomes generated by an insurance market dominated by consumer misinformation, there exist other explanations for the existence of differing deductible policy offerings. For example, if different endowment points are allowed in the R-S-W model firms may have additional incentives for offering deductible policies. That is, given identical utility functions, a $100 deductible collision policy may not provide the same satisfaction for an owner of a $30,000 Mercedes-Benz as it provides for an owner of a $5000 Honda Civic. A payment of $100 of collision coverage is obviously a more significant portion of a $5000 coverage policy than a $30,000 coverage policy. Thus, a Mercedes-Benz owner may desire a higher deductible policy (e.g., $600 deductible) in order to experience the same satisfaction as a Honda Civic owner purchasing a $100 deductible policy. Hence, some firms may offer a menu of low deductible policies (e.g., $100, $200) in an attempt to service economy car (Honda) owners, while other firms offer a menu of high deductible policies (e.g., $200, $600) in an attempt to service luxury car (Mercedes-Benz) owners.

Another reason for the existence of varying deductible policies might be attributed to the violation of the Wilson equilibrium assumption employed throughout the analyses. That is some firms, in an attempt to earn short-run profits, may behave in a Nash sense (short-sided) and offer policies that earn short-run profits even though in the long-run these policies are destined to incur significant losses. And finally, varying degrees of customer risk aversion may also help explain the existence of differing deductible policies.

Figure 3.11 below helps explain the observed menu of automobile insurance policies in terms of the R-S-W model. The diagram depicts the usual contract lines EL and EH for low-risk and high-risk individuals respectively. In the absence of consumer misinformation, firms offer the separating contract set $(\alpha^H, \alpha^{L'})$. However, for automobile insurance coverage, differing deductible policies set at different rates are observed. To depict this situation in the diagram consider how the presence of consumer misinformation problems alters firm behavior. For example, a firm may now offer low-risk individuals more coverage (lower deductibles) than they receive with purchasing contract $\alpha^{L'}$. Denote this new coverage policy as contract c_1 on line EL. However, if contract c_1 is offered, high-risk individuals favor purchasing it instead of α^H since they experience more satisfaction purchasing c_1. The presence of consumer misinformation now comes into play. If only a fraction of high-risk individuals are aware of the c_1 contract offering

TABLE 3.1

The Aetna Casualty and Surety Company Semi-Annual Auto-Rite
Base Premiums*

Territory 1 Age Group	1,2	3	4	5	6	7	8	10	11	12	13	14
			Symbol Group									

Full Coverage Comprehensive

	1,2	3	4	5	6	7	8	10	11	12	13	14
1	39	52	65	87	113	142						
2,3	30	39	49	66	85	107						
4,5	22	29	36	48	62	78						
6	18	24	30	40	52	64						

$100 Deductible Comprehensive

	1,2	3	4	5	6	7	8	10	11	12	13	14
1	28	37	46	62	80	100						
2,3	21	28	35	46	60	75						
4,5	16	21	26	34	44	55						
6	13	17	21	28	37	46						

$100 Deductible Collision

	1,2	3	4	5	6	7	8	10	11	12	13	14
1	74	83	98	118	137	157	167	186	206	225	245	314
2,3	55	63	74	88	103	118	125	140	155	170	184	235
4,5	48	54	64	76	89	102	109	122	134	147	160	204
6	40	46	54	65	75	86	92	103	114	124	135	172

$200 Deductible Collision

	1,2	3	4	5	6	7	8	10	11	12	13	14
1	64	72	86	104	122	140	150	168	186	204	223	286
2,3	46	53	64	77	90	104	111	125	138	152	166	213
4,5	40	46	54	66	78	89	95	108	120	131	143	184
6	33	38	45	55	65	75	80	90	100	110	120	155

*The Aetna Casualty and Surety Company Semi-Annual Auto-Rite
Base Premiums for the state of New Jersey, effective October
17, 1981. Submitted to the New Jersey Insurance Commission.

TABLE 3.2

Travelers Insurance Company Semi-Annual Base Premiums*

Territory 1 Age Group	1,2	3	Symbol Codes 4	5	6	7	8
No Deductible Comprehensive
1	42	53	72	93	117	130	
2,3	32	40	54	70	87	97	
4,5	23	29	39	51	64	71	
6	19	24	32	42	52	58	
$50 Deductible Comprehensive
1	34	42	57	74	92	103	
2,3	25	32	43	55	69	77	
4,5	18	23	31	40	51	57	
6	15	19	26	33	42	46	
$100 Deductible Collision
1	83	98	118	137	157	167	
2,3	62	74	88	103	118	125	
4,5	54	64	76	89	102	108	
6	46	54	65	75	86	92	
$250 Deductible Collision
1	63	74	89	104	118	126	
2,3	47	56	67	78	89	94	
4,5	41	48	58	67	77	82	
6	35	41	49	57	65	69	

*Travelers Insurance Semi-Annual premiums, effective September 16, 1981. Submitted to the New Jersey Insurance Commission.

TABLE 3.3
Prudential Property and Casualty Insurance Co. Private
Passenger Automobile Six-Month Premiums[*]

Territory 1

Age Group	Symbol Codes 1,2	3	4	5	6	7
			$50 Deductible Comprehensive			
1	70	70	87	104	144	178
2,3	59	59	74	89	122	151
4,5	52	52	65	78	108	134
6 & Over	38	38	48	57	79	98
			$100 Deductible Comprehensive			
1	46	46	57	68	94	117
2,3	39	39	48	58	80	99
4,5	34	34	43	58	80	88
6 & Over	25	25	31	38	52	64
			$200 Deductible Collision			
1	96	96	107	118	139	161
2,3	82	82	91	101	119	137
4,5	67	67	75	82	97	112
6 & Over	54	54	59	65	77	89

[*]Prudential Property and Casualty Insurance Company Private
Passenger Automobile Six-Month Premiums, New Jersey,
effective September 22, 1981. Submitted to the New Jersey
Insurance Commission.

TABLE 3.4

Insurance Services Office Personal Auto Manual Premium Rates[*]

Territory 1

Age	Symbol Group					
Group	5	6	7	8	10/J	11/K

$50 Deductible Comprehensive

	5	6	7	8	10/J	11/K
1	103	142	176	210	262	317
2,3	88	121	149	178	222	271
4,5	77	106	132	158	197	239
6	57	78	97	116	144	175

$100 Deductible Comprehensive

	5	6	7	8	10/J	11/K
1	82	113	140	167	208	253
2,3	70	96	119	142	277	216
4,5	62	84	105	125	157	190
6	45	62	77	93	115	139

$200 Deductible Collision

	5	6	7	8	10/J	11/K
1	187	221	254	290	324	357
2,3	161	189	217	247	275	305
4,5	131	155	180	202	226	251
6	105	123	142	161	180	198

[*]Insurance Services Office, New Jersey Rate Personal
Auto Manual, Copyright 1981.

then only this fraction of high-risk individuals purchase c_1.
Thus, a firm offering c_1, now is servicing low-risk and a fraction of high-risk individuals.   It then   revises its costs of
servicing these individuals and raises price accordingly.   Let
line EL_1 represent the actuarially fair contract line for servicing these individuals.   Contract c_2 then is offered on line
EL_1.   If consumer misinformation persists, contract c_2 is a
viable contract offering since firms that offer it do not incur
losses. Hence, in a market plagued by consumer misinformation,
one firm may offer contract α^L , while another firm offers contract c_2.   The contracts differ with respect to both coverage
levels (deductible level) and price.

Firms may also   deviate from   the $\alpha^{L'}$ coverage   level by
offering contract c_3 on line EL_2. To see this notice that contract c_3 lies on the high-risk group's indifference curve U^H so
that high-risk individuals continue purchasing α^H.   Thus, if
there are some low-risk individuals unaware of the $\alpha^{L'}$ offering they now purchase   contract c_3 at an increased   price (reflected by line EL_2). Firms offering c_3 earn short-run profits
until non-price competition drives profits to zero.   Again,
competing in the same marketplace, firms may differ in their
policy offerings as revealed by contract offerings $\alpha^{L'}$ and
c_3.

The presence of consumer misinformation problems makes it
difficult to assess regulatory effects on insurance policy
offerings.   Consumer misinformation inhibits market discipline
such that a firm's decision on the composition of its policy
offerings is not as sensitive to other firm's policy offerings
than the sensitivity that would exist in a market free of consumer misinformation problems. Firms, then, may be free to
pursue their desire of marketing uniform deductible policies
across states without the threat of market discipline.   And it
appears that firms choose to offer a certain menu of deductible
policies in the market and adhere to this menu whether they are
in a regulated or competitive state.   Indeed, as David Foster,
Director of Planning and Research of the Prudential Property
and Casualty Insurance Company states, "There are many reasons
(e.g., agent training, sales promotion material, servicing,
computer systems, pricing) why we try to keep deductible
options as uniform as possible from state to state."[23]   And in
addition, some states require all firms to offer a set menu of
deductible options.   For example, in New York the deductible
options which must be offered are: for comprehensive coverage
-$50, $200, $500, and $1000 deductible and for collision coverage - $100, $200, $250, $500, and $1000 deductible.[24] Insurers
may offer other deductible levels in addition to those set
forth above.   Thus, the presence of consumer misinformation
problems, the desire for uniform policies   across states
(because of the transaction costs associated with differing
policies), and the enforcement by some states for uniform

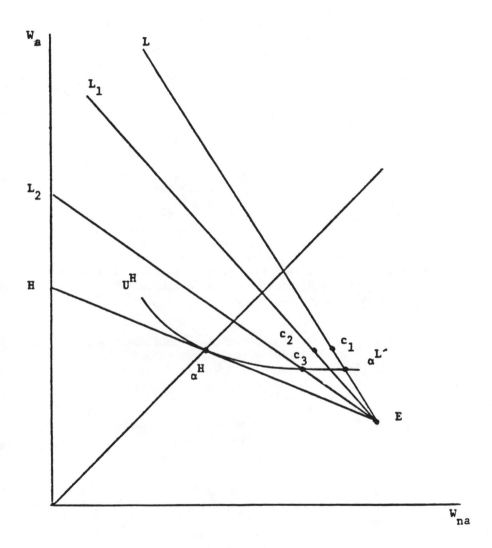

FIGURE 3.11

73

deductible options   across firms   makes it difficult   to assess
regulatory effects on policy offerings.

In summation, observations in the   property-liability insurance industry (i.e., automobile insurance) are inconclusive
in that they do not firmly support some of the hypotheses
generated from the analyses (e.g., regulatory effects). On the
other hand, observations do not reject the hypotheses either.
Insurance market observations are consistent with the notion
that the presence of consumer misinformation problems and insurance regulations disturb the insurance markets' way of dealing with adverse selection problems. However, the effects of
consumer misinformation and other factors (i.e., transaction
costs of altering deductible options and enforcement of uniform
deductible options across firms) appear to weigh more heavily
on market outcomes than regulatory effects.

THE MERITS OF GOVERNMENT REGULATION

This section offers a discussion on whether government
regulations provide a useful service for society and discusses
a possible alternative arrangement to the present regulatory
scheme.   Basically, reasons for regulation are tied to the
nature of the insurance business which makes desirable some
basis for assuring that insurers will be financially solvent so
they can keep their promises made to customers.   The ensuing
discussion, then, emphasizes the importance of securing a
financially sound insurance industry.   More specifically, the
government stated goals of insurance regulation are employed to
assess the merits of government intervention. The goals of insurance regulation are to assure:

1. the lowest possible rates consistent
    with underlying costs.
2. the continued solvency of insurance
    companies so that they can meet their
    future obligations,
    and
3. the continued availability of needed
    insurance coverages.[25]

In terms of the R-S-W model, the first goal is interpreted
to be consistent with firms offering the appropriate insurance
policies (i.e., separating or pooling contracts), that are
necessary to combat adverse selection problems, at actuarially
fair prices.   The second goal is consistent with the stability
of insurance firms' operations (i.e., the variability in
profits and losses).   And the third goal is consistent with
consumers purchasing their desired coverage levels and, more

importantly, firms offering some insurance coverage to all consumers.

The findings from this chapter suggest that it is important to assess the effects of government intervention in the context of information problems. Indeed, besides the direct and obvious effects of regulation (e.g., higher prices and lower coverage levels), government intervention has other significant effects on insurance market outcomes. For example, rate regulation may disturb the insurance market's way of dealing with information problems. Rate regulation may alter a market's policy offerings in that firms may switch from offering pooling contracts to offering separating contracts or vice versa, depending on the riskiness composition of individuals in the market. Also under a prior approval system, regulation impairs a firm's ability to respond to and even detect changing market conditions and thus results in less stable insurance firm operations. Finally, coverage restrictions may indirectly force firms to drop their separating contracts in favor of pooling contracts.

It is important to note that these indirect effects of government intervention are side effects and are not related to the expressed goals of regulation. So what are the merits of government intervention? Specifically, do government interventions, such as rate regulation and minimum coverage requirements, provide a useful service for society or can a non-regulated market perform just as well, or even better?

The literature (e.g., Joskow (53), MacAvoy (68), and the Virginia Insurance Commission Report (111)) suggests that a non-regulated competitive insurance market is better equipped to fulfill the three stated goals of regulation than a regulated insurance market. Insurance market studies conclude that insurance regulation results in higher priced contracts, less stable insurance market operations, and supply shortages. This study's examinations support these findings and as stated earlier, find other side effects of government intervention that corroborate what other insurance market studies have found, namely that regulated insurance markets are not equipped to meet the stated goals of regulation. However, this does not imply that a non-regulated competitive insurance market is the best alternative. Information problems do exist (e.g., consumer misinformation and informational asymmetries) in insurance markets and appropriate government interventions might improve market outcomes. Also, even though findings suggest that a competitive insurance market provides for a more stable insurance system than a regulated market, this does not imply that there is no solvency problem. Recall, that because of the nature of the insurance business, emphasis is placed on the importance of securing a financially sound insurance industry. Thus, government intervention might have a place in providing security for a financially sound insurance industry.

An Alternative Arrangement

An alternative arrangement to the present regulatory
scheme now is discussed. Let us begin with the understanding
that a competitive insurance market best fulfills the stated
goals of regulation and that consequently use of government
intervention be restricted to improving market outcomes in
light of information problems or securing a financially sound
insurance industry. Of course, the two areas are critically
related; the market's inabilities to deal with information
problems impairs the financial stability of the insurance industry. Thus, if government intervention can improve upon the
market's information problems, it also is contributing to the
financial soundness of the industry. Government intervention
of this kind affects the risk classification process which is
examined in Chapter 4.

As stated throughout this chapter, informational asymmetries in insurance markets result in the market offering either
pooling or separating contracts, depending on the composition
of low- and high-risk individuals in the market. Figure 3.2
depicts this situation with the market offering the separating
equilibrium (α^H, α^{L-}) when the market fair individuals in the
market. Figure 3.2 depicts this situation with the market offering the separating equilibrium (α^H, α^{L-}) when the market fair
odds line is EF and the market offering the pooling W equilibrium when the market fair odds line is EF'. If the separating contract (α^H, α^{L-}) is offered, the only Pareto move would
arise if the high-risk group revealed themselves. In this case,
the low-risk group can be made better off purchasing contract
α^L, while the high-risk group continues to purchase α^H. Forcing firms to offer a pooling contract is not a Pareto move
since the zero-profit pooling contract lies on line EF which
results in the low-risk group being made worse-off (since line
EF lies below U^{L-}). Also forcing firms to offer more insurance
coverage to the low-risk group is not a Pareto-move since this
is, in effect, a binding minimum coverage restriction on the
low-risk group. And as Section 3.4 clearly demonstrates,
minimum coverage requirements result in firms offering pooling
contracts on line EF in Figure 3.2.[26] Thus, when a
separating equilibrium exists, government intervention should
be limited to the role of an information center. That is, the
government would serve society best by providing the necessary
information (data) to improve firms' abilities to identify the
high-risk group.

If the pooling equilibrium W exists, so that line EF'
represents the market fair odds line in Figure 3.2, the government's involvement is still limited to the role of an information center. To see this, notice that the low-risk group's
indifference curve, U_1^L is tangent to line EF'. It then follows, that if the government forces firms to offer a pooling
contract that offers more coverage (moving W to the left along

line EF´) the low-risk group is made worse-off. Similarly, if the government forces firms to offer separating contracts (i.e., (α^H, $\alpha^{L´}$)) the low-risk group is made worse-off. Thus the only Pareto-move would be for the government to provide the necessary information so that firms can identify the high-risk group and consequently offer the (α^H, α^L) set.[27]

The government's role as an information center also is consistent with improving insurance market outcomes when consumer misinformation problems prevail. The section under that heading clearly demonstrates that firms take advantage of consumer misinformation by altering coverage levels, the types of policies offered and the price charged for insurance coverage. A government information service designed to facilitate comparative policy shopping, then, improves market outcomes.

The importance of securing a financially sound insurance industry is the ultimate goal of government intervention. However, as this chapter suggests, it is important that government intervention, focused on the industry solvency problems, does not interfere with the competitive market's way of handling information problems.[28] Further, government intervention designed to promote financial stability must depend in part on the acceptance of market forces as a mechanism for weeding out weak and poorly managed firms. Solvency regulations are of this type which acts to keep firm solvency in check while permitting some firms the opportunity to fail. However, a government fund must be established to pay off unearned premiums of the failed firms to customers. For these reasons the government might better develop a system in which the financial soundness of the insurance industry is assured by a Federal Property-Liability Insurance Corporation (FPLIC).[29] This would be a parallel insurance system similar to the relationship between the Federal Deposit Insurance Corporation (FDIC) and commercial banks. Under such a system, insurance firms would be required to join the federal property-liability insurance system, and pay premiums for insurance coverage to fully insure their unearned premiums.[30] Premiums could be based on the total unearned premiums of each firm, similar to the FDIC arrangement, or it could be based on the associated risk of each insurance firm.[31] In return for insurance coverage, property-liability firms would be subject to federal solvency regulations designed to promote stable insurance firm operations.[32] And similar to FDIC operations, the FPLIC would monitor property-liability firm operations and would be empowered with the tools to prevent firm insolvency, such as providing loans to the troubled firm or allowing mergers between a failing firm and a healthy firm. And if the FPLIC allows a firm to fail, it pays off the firm's customers (the amount of unearned premiums) from an insurance fund created by premium paid in by the property-liability firms.

A Federal Property-Liability Insurance Corporation alternative to today's insurance regulations seems to be a sensible and viable solution. An FPLIC arrangement would allow the competitive insurance market to operate freely in the pricing and marketing of its policies and to deal with market information problems, while assuring a financially sound industry through insurance coverage. The FPLIC also can play another major role in improving insurance market outcomes. It can act as an information center for the insurance industry. And since all property-liability firms are members of the FPLIC, it is in a position to gather a great deal of insurance information. Requiring firms to submit their policies with corresponding coverages, prices, and risk classifications provides the FPLIC with an enormous data base with which to conduct insurance market research in an effort to improve the market's abilities to deal with inherent information problems. The FPLIC also can publish effective policy guides to facilitate comparative policy shopping, a problem exposed in a previous section.

SUMMARY AND CONCLUSIONS

This chapter assessed the effects of government intervention on insurance market outcomes in the context of information problems. The findings suggest that today's regulations, such as rate regulation under the prior approval system and minimum coverage requirements, may affect insurance market outcomes beyond direct and obvious effects. For example, rate regulations, besides creating higher priced policies, may disturb the insurance market's way of dealing with information problems. Rate regulation may alter a market's policy offerings in that firms may switch from offering pooling contracts to offering separating contracts or vice versa, depending on the riskiness composition of individuals in the market. And under a prior approval system, regulation impairs a firm's ability to respond to and even to detect changing market conditions and thus results in less stable insurance firm operations. Also, coverage restrictions may indirectly force firms to drop their separating contracts in favor of pooling contracts. Finally, the importance of assessing the effects of consumer misinformation on market outcomes in the context of informational asymmetries is stressed. Firms can take advantage of consumer misinformation by altering coverage levels, the type of policies offered, and the price charged for insurance coverage.

The analyses suggest that government intervention designed to improve market outcomes should take the market's information problems into account. A competitive pricing arrangement is necessary to satisfy the traditional goals of regulation, and if government intervention interferes with the workings of a free market it could be damaging. Indeed, the government is seen only in the limited role as an information center. Also government intervention designed to promote financial stability should take the form of a federal insurance system. Specifi-

cally, property-liability insurance firms should   purchase federal insurance to guarantee their unearned premiums.   In this
way customers are   assured that   they will   either   receive the
product they   purchased (insurance   coverage) or they   will receive the dollar amount on the unearned premium paid for future
insurance coverage in case of firm insolvency.

In conclusion, possible problems in the accident insurance
market are   due primarily   to information problems   and today's
insurance regulations.   Government   intervention,   then, must
be designed with   the purpose   of not   only   promoting industry
stability, but to   improve the   market's ability   to   deal with
information problems.   It is also true, that in the absence of
government intervention, firms can also   alleviate information
problems   by expending resources to classify   individuals into
their appropriate risk classes.   The effects of risk classification on market outcomes are now examined in Chapter 4.

APPENDIX A

The equation of line EL in Figure 3.1 can be derived by recognizing that W_a, W_{na} is a probability space. Let us use the following information:

(a_1)
$$W_{na} = W - \pi^L q$$

(a_2)
$$W_a = W - L + (1-\pi^L)q$$

(a_3)
$$(1-p^L)\,\pi^L q - p^L(1-\pi^L)q = 0 \ .$$

Equations (a_1) and (a_2) are low-risk individuals' expected wealth in the no-accident and accident states respectively, if they choose to participate in the insurance process and equation (a_3) is a competitive firm's zero-profit constraint for selling low-risk insurance. Solving the zero-profit constraint for $(1-\pi^L)q$ yields

(a_4)
$$(1-\pi^L)q = \frac{(1-p^L)}{p^L}\,\pi^L q.$$

Plugging (a_4) into (a_2) results in

(a_5)
$$W_a = W-L + \frac{(1-p^L)}{p^L}\,\pi^L q$$

and from equation (a_1) we know that

(a_6)
$$\pi^L q = W - W_{na} \ .$$

Inserting (a_6) into (a_5) leaves us with

(a_7)
$$W_a = W - L + \frac{(1-p^L)}{p^L}(W - W_{na}).$$

Rearranging equation (a_7) yields

(a_8)
$$W_a = \frac{(1-p^L)}{p^L}\,W + W-L - \frac{(1-p^L)}{p^L}\,W_{na}.$$

Recognizing that $\dfrac{p^L}{p^L}\,W = W$, (a_8) reduces to

(a_9)
$$W_a = \frac{W}{p^L} - L - \frac{(1-p^L)}{p^L} W_{na},$$

and since the zero-profit constraint (a_3) implies

(a_{10})
$$\frac{(1-p^L)}{p^L} = \frac{(1-\pi^L)}{\pi^L},$$

the equation of a low-risk contract offer line, such as line EL in Figure 3.1, is

(a_{11})
$$W_a = \frac{W}{p^L} - L - \frac{(1-\pi^L)}{\pi^L} W_{na}$$

where $-\dfrac{(1-\pi^L)}{\pi^L}$ is the slope. A similar analysis for the high-risk group results in the high-risk contract offer line

(a_{12})
$$W_a = \frac{W}{\rho^H} - L - \frac{(1-\pi^H)}{\pi^H} W_{na}.$$

APPENDIX B

The addition of administrative costs to a firm's expect-ed profits alters the basic expected profit equation, such as equation (5), so that

$$(b_1) \qquad\qquad (1-p) \; \pi\,qn - p(1-\pi)qn - c(n),$$

where administrative costs, $c(n)$, is an increasing function of the number of policies, n, sold by the firms, becomes the firm's expected profits. Thus expected revenue now depends on the number of policies sold. Similarly, expected costs depend on the number of policies sold as well.

A long-run competitive equilibrium forces expected profits to zero, which after some manipulation (b_1) becomes

$$(b_2) \qquad\qquad \frac{\pi}{1-\pi} = \frac{p}{1-p} + \frac{c(n)}{(1-p)(1-\pi)qn}.$$

Equation (b_2) states that the price of insurance $\pi/1-\pi$ is greater than the actuarially fair price by the term $c(n)/(1-p)(1-\pi)qn$. Individuals facing a price of insurance no long-er corresponding to their probabilities of accident will not fully insure. The proof is as follows:

From equation (3.3) we have

$$(b_3) \qquad\qquad \frac{U'(W-L + (1-\pi)q)}{U'(W-\pi\,\upsilon)} \; \frac{(1-p)}{p} = \frac{\pi}{1-\pi}.$$

Substituting (b_2) into (b_3) yields

$$(b_4) \qquad\qquad \frac{U'(W-L + (1-\pi)q)}{U'(W-\pi q)} = 1 + \frac{c(n)}{p(1-\pi)qn}.$$

Setting $1 = \dfrac{p(1-\pi)qn}{p(1-\pi)qn}$ yields

$$(b_5) \qquad\qquad \frac{U'(W-L + (1-\pi)q)}{U'(W-\pi q)} = \frac{p(1-\pi)qn + c(n)}{p(1-\pi)qn}.$$

Multiplying through results in

$$(b_6) \qquad U'(W-L +(1-\pi)q) \, (p(1-\pi)qn) = U'(W-\pi q) \, (p(1-\pi)qn+c(n))$$

since utility is independent of the state we are left with

$$(b_7) \qquad\qquad qp(1-\pi)qn - L = -\pi q c(n).$$

Solving for q will give us

$$(b_8) \qquad q = L \; \frac{1}{p(1-\pi)qn} - \frac{\pi qc(n)}{p(1-\pi)qn}.$$

Equation (b_8) tells us that coverage q is equal to some fraction of expected loss, L, minus the term $\pi qc(n)/p(1-\pi)qn$ which can be shown to be positive. The numerator $\pi qc(n) > 0$ since πq is the premium and $c(n)$ is administrative costs which are both assumed to be greater than zero. The denominator $p(1-\pi)qn$ is the firms expected cost which is obviously positive. Thus the amount of coverage desired is less than the expected loss.

It now can be easily shown that in a regulated market where $\pi_R > \pi$, individuals will purchase less coverage than in the case above. Recall, that the amount of coverage purchased for the above case was derived from (b_4). The right-hand side of of (b_4) is greater than 1 and thus if the equation is to hold, $U'(W-L-(1-\pi)q) > U'(W-\pi q)$. Employing the approach described in the second section of this chapter, coverage q will decrease until (b_4) holds. Thus coverage will decrease until it satisfies condition (b_8). However, under regulation, $\pi_R > \pi$, it follows that the the right hand term in (b_4), $c(n)/p(1-\pi)qn$ increases in value. Thus in order for (b_4) to hold under regulation, coverage must be decreased by an even greater amount than is satisfied by condition (b_8).

NOTES

1. For the past two decades there has been discussion among insurance commissions and academists whether or not to abolish rate regulation. And some states have recently eliminated rate regulation, e.g., California and Virginia.

2. Thus explicit solvency regulations are ignored, e.g., asset restrictions and capital requirements. This leaves rate regulation as the sole protection of firm solvency in the model; see Chapter 1, second section.

3. Administrative costs are assumed away for expositional simplicity. They can easily be included and shown not to change the direction of our results. See Appendix B for further analysis.

4. See Chapter 2 for relevant background material.

5. See Appendix A for derivation of equation for offer lines.

6. Informational asymmetries are chosen because it is the most common information problem examined in the literature. However, other information problems also exist, such as moral hazard and inaccurate information. Also the problems of moral hazard are assumed away for simplicity, and the problems of inaccurate information are dealt with partly in other sections of this chapter and parts of Chapter 4.

7. A Wilson equilibrium was first employed in Wilson (111). It has been used in insurance market analysis ever since, e.g., Kleindorfer and Kunreuther (59) and Hoy (49).

8. Both Joskow (53) and the Virginia Insurance Commission report (111) report these findings.

9. Joskow (53).

10. Virginia Insurance Commission Report (111), page 13.

11. Ibid.

12. Obviously, other differences between a regulated and competitive insurance market exist, e.g., the risks a regulated firm faces may differ from the risks a competitive firm faces since the objective of rate regulation is to protect firm solvency.

13. Obviously, individuals will not fully insure in the non-regulated case if administrative costs are considered. In Appendix B, it is demonstrated that whether the non-regulated benchmark is full insurance or partial insurance, regulating price will further reduce the individual's desired coverage level.

14. The elimination of profits partly can be attributed to non-price competition and partly to scale economies which cause firms to move to the left of the minimum point on their average cost curves as more firms enter the market.

15. Virginia Insurance Commission Report (111), page 17.

16. We shall dispense with an examination of price flexibility from an initial separating equilibrium. The examination involves too many outcomes to give the analysis credibility,

not to mention its incomprehensibility with graphical exposition.

17. The position of the pooling contract W_1 on line EF_1 is determined by maximizing the benefits of the low-risk group. However, the rate change does not represent an increase to the low-risk group. This is because lines EF and EF_1 represent the actuarially fair odds line for the pooled group. Thus, the low-risk group will not reduce coverage in response to a price increase.

18. Of course there exists the possibility that the increased riskiness could result in a separating equilibrium. That is, line EF_1 could lie to the left of the low-risk group's indifference curve passing through the α^L point. However, we assume this possibility cannot occur so that we may focus our examination only on the effects of prior approval.

19. The contract set is a Nash equilibrium, but as we now demonstrate, not a Wilson equilibrium.

20. The effects of minimum coverage requirements are illustrated from an initial pooling equilibrium in this footnote since the results are trivial. In the following diagram, if the pooling equilibrium is contract W then the minimum coverage constraint q^*m is binding. Thus firms are forced to offer the pooling contract W^*. In this binding case, coverage requirements force individuals to purchase more insurance coverage.

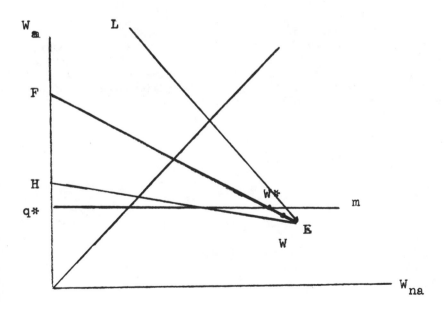

21. Kunreuther discusses the Cummins and Kunreuther surveys in a comment in Munch and Smallwood (79).

22. The FTC was working on such a yardstick to measure
policies by until Congress prohibited FTC involvement with the
insurance industry.

23. David Foster's statement was obtained from a written
interview I conducted with him on November 15, 1982.

24. Circular Letter No. 13, state of New York Insurance
Department, November 3, 1977.

25. Virginia Insurance Commission Report (111), page iii.

26. Of course, as the section on minimum coverage
restrictions points out, there are other important reasons for
imposing minimum coverage requirements.

27. This is a Pareto-optimal move even though the high-
risk group is made worse-off (going from W to α^H) because the
product (insurance) has changed. In other words, the high-risk
group, if identified, becomes a higher-priced insurance product
and purchasing α^H benefits society since they purchase actuarially fair contracts.

28. For example, this chapter shows how today's insurance
regulations designed to assure industry stability, produces adverse side effects on market outcomes. Regulations may alter
the market's policy offerings, price charged on policies, and
coverage levels.

29. A similar type of alternative insurance arrangement
is recommended in MacAvoy (68).

30. Specifically, each firm will have an expected average
for unearned premiums for a given year.

31. A premium system based on firm risk is clearly
superior to one based on firm deposits (i.e., unearned premiums). See Chapter 5.

32. Of course these solvency regulations are already in
effect. I propose that they be all placed under the auspices
of the FPLIC. However, other regulations, such as minimum coverage requirements, compulsory insurance, licensing of agents,
etc., may still be enforced by state regulations since each
state has a different insurance environment.

4

Accident Risk Classification

INTRODUCTION

This chapter focuses on an activity that firms participate in when informational asymmetries exist, the grouping of individuals into risk classes. In a competitive insurance market, firms have incentive to expend resources to learn to distinguish low-risk and high-risk individuals, because if firms can distinguish at a low enough cost, there are profits to be made. Thus, firms have incentive to alleviate adverse selection problems by classifying individual risks.

The objective in this chapter is to examine the role of risk classification and assess its effects on insurance market outcomes. The chapter proceeds in the following steps. The first part examines the effects of the risk classification process in the R-S-W model developed in Chapter 3. The analysis reveals that a firm is more likely to further define risk classes when the market initially offers separating contracts than when the market initially offers pooling contracts. Findings also indicate that firms pass on the cost of classification only to the low-risk group. A comparative analysis of two risk classification schemes, a rating bureau's classifications, and an independent firm's classifications are then presented. Allowing for differing classification accuracies between the two schemes, the examinations reveal that from initial pooling contracts, inaccurate classification results in ineffective market outcomes, while from initial separating contracts, inaccurate classification results in efficient market outcomes. Also depending on the level of accuracy, the bureau scheme may offer pooling contracts, while the independent scheme offers

separating contracts, or vice versa. And, surprisingly,
in some cases the more inaccurate the independent classification scheme, the better chance it has to compete with a more
accurate bureau classification scheme. Finally, a discussion
on the risk classification process for automobile insurance and
how both competitive and regulated insurance environments deal
with the risk classification process is offered. The discussion suggests that a competitive environment results in more
accurate risk classifications than a regulated environment's
classification.

RISK CLASSIFICATION IN THE R-S-W MODEL

This section examines the effects of risk classification
on market outcomes in the R-S-W accident insurance model. Risk
classification is defined as an attempt by insurance firms to
categorize individuals into specific risk groups where differences in risk are defined as differences in probabilities of
incurring accident. And to distinguish among individual probabilities of accident, firms expend resources, time, and energy
to collect data in order to study, formulate, and test new risk
classifications.[1] Quantifying these efforts at risk classification, it is assumed a firm expends K dollars to create a
new risk class. For simplicity, assume K is a constant dollar
amount for any risk classification even though, in actuality,
each risk classification process is probably associated with a
different K.

The R-S-W two-state, accident, no accident, insurance
model previously presented in Chapter 3 will be employed. Thus,
the offering of the separating (α^H, α^L) and the pooling W contracts are the market's way of dealing with adverse
selection problems.[2] Figure 4.1 below depicts these two contract arrangements. It is obvious that if information were
perfect, in that firms were able to distinguish between low-
risk and high-risk individuals, a Pareto-improvement would
occur over the separating equilibrium by offering the contract
(α^H, α^L). Employing the same Pareto criteria, the same claim
cannot be made for the case of the pooling W equilibrium. Even
though low-risk individuals are made better off as a result of
perfect information (moving from W to α^L), a Pareto improvement
is not achieved since high-risk individuals are now worse off
at α^H. However, because of the nature of the insurance process, risk identification, in effect, changes the insurance
product. In other words, the high-risk group, if identified,
becomes a higher priced insurance product and purchasing α^H is
Pareto-optimal since they purchase actuarially fair contracts
at full insurance. Let us choose to label this Pareto-optimal
outcome efficient, since it represents customers purchasing
products (full insurance coverage) at a cost commensurate with

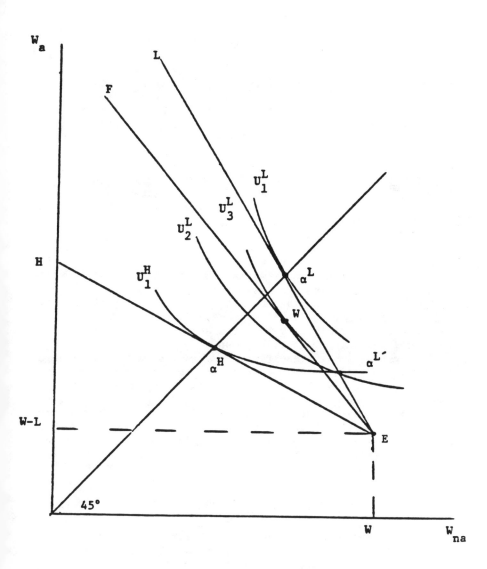

FIGURE 4.1

their risks. And if risk identification results in individuals
purchasing higher coverage contracts closer to their actuarially fair contract lines than before identification, this movement is said to be efficient. Thus, moving from W to (α^H, α^L)
as a result of perfect identification is efficient. Any risk
classification process resulting in a movement towards the
purchase of actuarially fair contracts is an improvement in
efficiency.

The process of risk classification in an insurance market
is illustrated in Figure 4.2 where low-risk and high-risk individuals start with an initial endowment (W, W-L) in an uninsured state at point E. Low-risk and high-risk actuarially
fair contract lines are placed in the diagram as EL and EH
respectively. Risk classification costs a firm a positive K
dollar amount. This additional cost of providing insurance is
a fixed cost and results in a leftward parallel shift of an
actuarially fair contract line. For example, a firm expending
K dollars to identify low-risk individuals in Figure 4.2 offers
a low-risk individual the contract line E_1L_1 which reflects the
additional K dollars of providing insurance. In effect, the
low-risk individual is offered a two-part tariff; he pays a
fixed K dollar amount for the privilege of being placed in the
low-risk group and then is offered a low-risk contract at an
actuarially fair rate. Thus, the identified low-risk individual's initial endowment is at E_1 since his initial wealth in
the no accident state is W-K and his initial wealth in the accident state is W-K-L. Notice that line E_1L_1 is a zero-profit
line because even though firms may earn short-run profits, free
entry tends to drive profits toward zero in the long-run.
Assuming perfect risk classification, the firm has effectively
segmented its market by allowing only low-risk individuals to
purchase on the E_1L_1 contract line and offering contract line
EH to the remaining high-risk group.

Imperfect risk classification results in a rotation of
line E_1L_1 to $E_1L_1^P$.[3] To see this, notice that imperfect classification causes line E_1L_1 no longer to be the actuarially fair
contract line for the 'perceived' low-risk group. There are now
some high-risk individuals that the firm perceives to be low-
risk. The perceived fair odds line for this low-risk group is
greater and subsequently lies to the left of the actual low-
risk group fair odds line, E_1L_1. And there are now some low-
risk individuals that the firm perceives to be high-risk so
that line EH^P becomes the perceived high-risk group's fair odds
line.

Obviously there exists a limit to the amount of dollars a
firm can expend on risk classification. Figure 4.3 illustrates
the dollar limits for the perfect risk classification case from
both pooling and separating equilibriums. Let us begin with
the offering of the pooling contract W so that the market fair
odds line EF lies to the right of the low-risk group's indifference curve, U_1^L, passing through point α^L. The cost con-

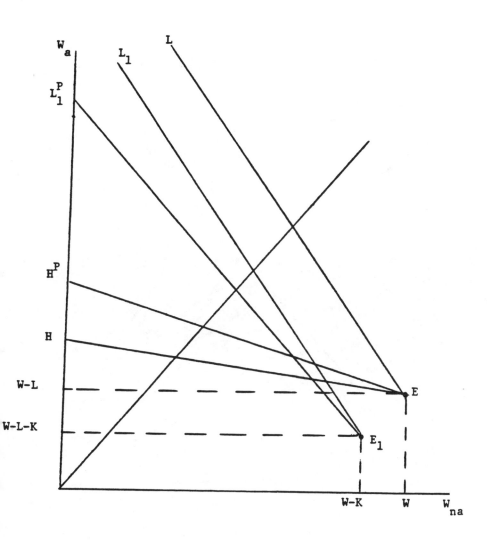

FIGURE 4.2

91

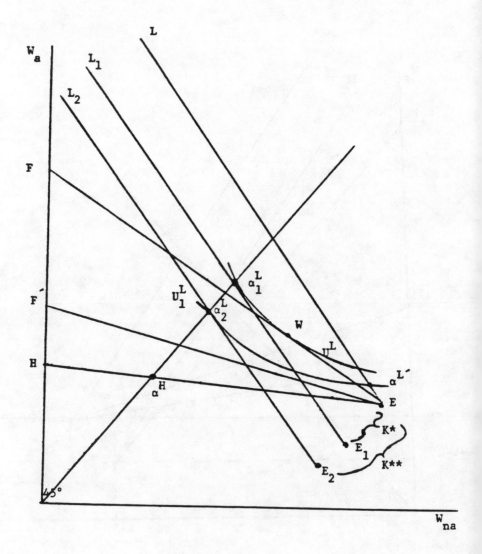

FIGURE 4.3

92

straint on the risk classification process is K^* which results
in the contract offer line E_1L_1 for the identified low-risk
group. To see this, notice that the identified low-risk group,
charged an actuarially fair price, purchases full insurance at
point α_1^L (where line E_1L_1 intersects the 45° line). Thus,
low-risk individuals are indifferent between being identified
as low-risk (purchasing a two-part tariff which results in contract α_1^L) or purchasing the pooling contract W since the low-
lowrisk group's indifference curve, U_1^L, for purchasing the pooling contract W, passes through point α^L. It follows then that
that K^* represents the dollar limit firms may expend on low-
risk classification because, for any $K>K^*$, the resulting contract offer line for the identified low-risk group lies to the
left of line E_1L_1 resulting in a loss in welfare for the identified low-risk group. Thus, if firms expend $K>K^*$, the low-
risk group always prefers the pooling W contract. If an initial
separating equilibrium exists, so that the market fair odds
line is EF^-, the contract set (α^H, α^{L^-}) is offered. The cost
constraint on low-risk classification is K^{**} dollars, for reasons similar to those given above. If firms expend K^{**} dollars,
line E_2L_2 is offered to the identified low-risk group. They
then fully insure at point α_2^L which also lies on the low-risk
group's indifference curve, U_1^L, that passes through point α^{L^-}.
As a result the low-risk group is indifferent between being
identified and participating in the two-part tariff scheme
(purchasing contract α_2^L) or participating in the self-selection
process (purchasing contract α^{L^-}). It follows that for any
$K>K^{**}$, the low-risk group prefers contract α^{L^-} to any contract
offered from the risk classification process.

The above demonstrates that firms may expend more money
(K^{**}) on risk classification from an initial separating equilibrium than from an initial pooling equilibrium (K^*). A bias
in the risk classification process exists in that firm participation in the risk classification process is more likely when
the market offers separating contracts than when the market
offers pooling contracts.

One final comment about how risk classification is represented in the R-S-W model should be made. It is claimed that
firms pass on the cost of risk classification directly to the
low-risk group. For example, in Figure 4.2, a firm expending
K dollars to identify low-risk individuals offers them the actuarially fair contract line E_1L_1, reflecting the total classification cost, K. The low-risk group, then, bears the total
cost of identification, while the remaining high-risk group,
i.e., individuals on fair odds line EH, does not. As Figure
4.4 below reveals, the low-risk group always bears the classification cost. To see this let us begin with the offering of
the pooling W contract so that the market fair odds line is EF.
Perfect classification results in the low- and high-risk contract offer lines E_1L_1 and EH respectively if firms pass on
the classification cost, K, directly to the identified low-risk

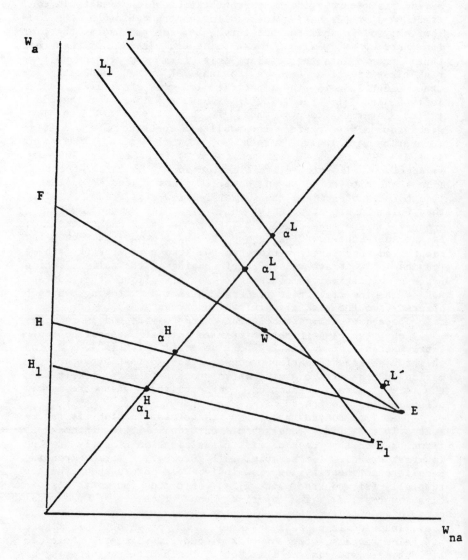

FIGURE 4.4

group. The market then offers the contract set (α^H, α_1^L). The non-negative profits (since the low-risk group prefers α_1^L to W). It is obvious that any firm that passes the classification cost, K, to the high-risk group eventually incurs losses. To see this, notice that line E_1 H_1 now is offered to the high-risk group reflecting the classification cost, K, so that lines E_1H_1 and EL are offered to the high- and low-risk groups re-respectively. The firm, then, offers the contract set (α_1^H, α^L) of which the high-risk group never purchases α_1^H since it always prefers α^H to it. Thus, firms offering the contract set (α_1^H, α^L) incur losses since no one purchases policy α_1^H and it costs firms an additional K dollars to offer α^L. It follows that any contract set that divides the classification cost between low- and high-risk groups is also not an equilibrium set, since the high-risk group always prefers their actuarially fair policy α^H to any contract that requires them, partially or completely, to bear the cost of classsification.[4]

DIFFERING CLASSIFICATION SCHEMES

Two risk classification schemes are now compared. First, a firm may independently classify risk at a cost K_I per classification. Alternatively, a firm may join a rating bureau and employ their risk classifications at a cost K_B per classification, where $K_B < K_I$. The bureau cost per classification is lower because the bureau pools information pertaining to risk classifications from many firms and consequently experiences economies of scale.

A firm then faces a choice of independently classifying risk at a cost K_I per classification or joining a rating bureau and paying K_B per classification. Obviously, a profit maximiz-ing firm will choose the alternative that results in greater expected profits. Then it would seem, all other things con-sidered equal, a firm will join the rating bureau since $K_B < K_I$ should allow greater expected profits with bureau classifica-tions. However, this assumes that both classification schemes possess the same level of accuracy in distinguishing individual risk and this may not be the case. It might be reasonable to assume that a rating bureau's classifications, based on the pooled experience of many firms, are more accurate than one firm's attempt at classifying risk. This is, indeed, true for the case of small insurance firms. Because of their size, they do not have the administrative or data collecting capabilities to compete with the much larger rating bureaus. On the other hand, a large insurance firm with an adequate data base might be better than the bureau at classifying risks in its own mar-kets and geographic regions. It is possible that in relying on bureau classifications, a large firm may sacrifice some accuracy. All of these possibilities are considered.

Outcomes in a competitive insurance market for the bureau and independent schemes with accurate classification are

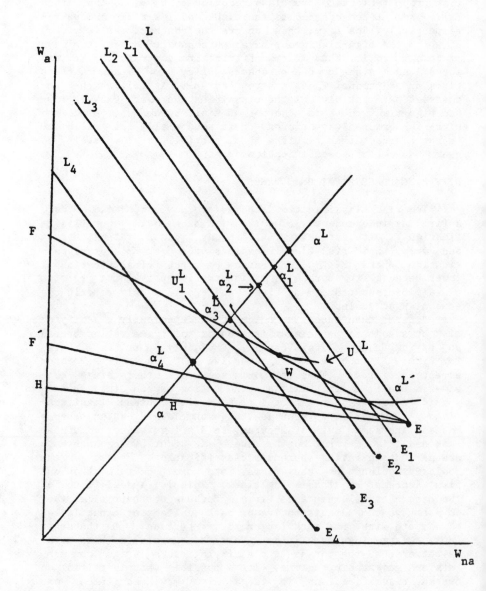

Figure 4.5

illustrated in Figure 4.5. The market is divided into two risk
groups, low-risk and high-risk, with corresponding actuarially
fair contract lines EL and EH. If firms are unable to identify
low-risk individuals the market will reach either the separating equilbrium ($\alpha^H, \alpha^{L'}$) or the pooling equilibrium, W, depending on the composition of low-risk and high-risk individuals in
the market. Let us begin with the pooling equilibrium, W,
assuming a low proportion of high-risk individuals represented
by the market fair odds line EF. Recall that there are two
risk classification schemes: independent and bureau. Firms
expend K_B dollars under the bureau scheme and K_I dollars under
the independent scheme, where $K_B < K_I$.

Bureau risk classification results in firms offering the
contract α_1^L on line E_1L_1 only to low-risk individuals and contract α^H on line EH to high-risk (other) individuals. To see
this, consider the changes that occur in Figure 4.5 as a result
of the classification process. Firms now can identify all low-
risk individuals because of the classification process, and
offers a contract to them on the EL fair odds line. However,
firms offer contract line E_1L_1 instead of EL to the low-risk
group to reflect the added cost of classification, K_B. Low-risk
and high-risk individuals, then, fully insure by purchasing
actuarially fair contracts, α^L and α^H respectively.

The contract set (α^H, α_1^L) is an equilibrium because any
firm continuing to sell the pooling contract W incurs losses
since the low-risk group prefers α_1^L to W. Thus, bureau classification makes high-risk individuals worse off (going from W
to α^H) and low-risk individuals better off (going from W to α_1^L)
in the traditional Pareto sense. However, the classification
process is efficient since both low-risk and high-risk groups
purchase full insurance on their actuarially fair contract
lines.

Independent risk classification results in firms identifying low-risk individuals on contract line E_2L_2 which is to the
left of line E_1L_1 in Figure 4.5 since $K_B < K_I$. And for reasons
similar to the bureau case, market equilibrium results in the
set of contract offerings (α^H, α_2^L). Independent classification,
then, from an initial pooling W equilibrium, is efficient
since both low- and high-risk groups purchase full insurance at
actuarially fair prices. However, the bureau scheme is clearly
a Pareto improvement over the independent scheme since the low-
risk group prefers α_1^L to α_2^L.

Of course it is possible that the cost of the independent
scheme is greater than the market's classification cost
constraint. For example, if independent classification costs a
firm K_I dollars such that contract line E_3L_3 is offered to the
low-risk group, the resulting contract offering set (α^H, α_3^L) is
not an equilibrium. To see this, notice that the low-risk group
prefers the the pooling W contract to the α_3^L contract since α_3^L
lies below the the low-risk group's indifference curve, U^{L_3},
tangent at point W. Thus firms offering the contract (α^H, α_3^L)

eventually incur losses. Perhaps this was the case during the early years of property-liability insurance. Individual firms were small, and because of their size did not have the administrative or data collecting capabilities to effectively classify risk, so they banded together to form rating bureaus.

The above examinations suggest that if firms can accurately classify risk, the bureau scheme is clearly superior to the independent scheme. Of course, this result is expected since $K_B < K_I$ was assumed and all other things remained the same. Nevertheless, it does suggest that if accurate risk classification is possible (or if the accuracy of classification is the same level for both the bureau and independent scheme) the insurance market is better off if firms band together and form rating bureaus rather than go it alone.

The effects of the risk classification process on market outcomes from an initial separating equilibrium are now considered. Assume that the market fair odds line is line EF' in Figure 4.5 which lies to the left of the low-risk group's indifference curve, U_I^L so that a separating equilibrium exists. From the above analysis, bureau classification results in the contract set (α^H, α_1^L) and independent classification results in the contract set (α^H, α_2^L). As was shown earlier, classification is efficient in both cases with the bureau scheme a Pareto improvement over the independent scheme. However, classification from a separating equilibrium also is a Pareto improvement in the traditional sense. Low-risk individuals are made better-off going from $\alpha^{L'}$ to α_2^L under the independent scheme and are even better-off going from $\alpha^{L'}$ to α_1^L under the bureau scheme, while high-risk individuals remain at α^H in both cases.

Of course there is the possibility that the cost of classifying customers by risk is greater than the market's classification cost limit. For example, if independent classification costs a firm K_1^* dollars, such that contract line $E_4 L_4$ is offered to the low-risk group, the resulting contract offering set (α^H, α_4^L) is not an equilibrium. For the low-risk group prefers $\alpha^{L'}$ to α_4^L (because α_4^L lies below U_I^L). Indeed, this result is consistent with the conclusion reached in Section 4.2; there exists a bias in the risk classification process in that firm participation in risk classification is more likely when the market offers separating contracts than when the market offers pooling contracts (since $K_1^* > K_1$ for the pooling case). The bias suggests that independent classification has a better chance of surviving when the market offers separating contracts than when the market offers pooling contracts.

Let us now examine the bureau and independent schemes when they inaccurately classify risk. First a general examination (no distinction between bureau and independent schemes is made) of the effects of imperfect risk classification on insurance market outcomes is illustrated in Figure 4.6 below. Figures 4.7 and 4.8 then depict the effects of imperfect risk classification for both the bureau and independent schemes.

Outcomes in a competitive insurance market with imperfect risk classification are illustrated in Figure 4.6. The examination begins with the pooling equilibrium at point W on the market fair odds line EF. Imperfect risk classification results in the firms offering the contract c_1 and line $E_1L_1^P$ to the perceived low-risk group and contract c_2 on line EH_2^P to the perceived high-risk group. To see this, notice that the perceived low-risk group's initial endowment now is at point E_1 since they must pay K dollars for being placed in the perceived low-risk group. However, since imperfect classification implies that there are some high-risk individuals in the perceived low-risk group, line E_1L_1 rotates to the left to reflect the riskiness of the perceived low-risk group. If line $E_1L_1^P$ represents the riskiness (fair odds line) of the perceived low-risk group, then firms maximize the actual low-risk individuals' benefits by offering contract c_1 which is the point of tangency of the actual low-risk group's indifference curve to line $E_1L_1^P$. Similarly, since there are some low-risk individuals placed in the perceived high-risk group, firms offer contract c_2 which is the point of tangency of the low-risk individuals' indifference curve to the perceived high-risk contract line EH^P. The contract set (c_2,c_1) is an equilibrium set. Any firm that offers the pooling W contract eventually incurs losses since the perceived low-risk group prefers c_1 to it. Thus imperfect classification can make the perceived low-risk individuals (the low-risk and high-risk individuals that are identified to be low-risk) better off (going from W to c_1) and the perceived high-risk individuals worse-off (going from W to c_2) in a Pareto sense. Imperfect risk classification also is not efficient, since even though the movement from W to c_1 is efficient (the perceived low-risk group is, in effect, a new risk group and they now purchase more coverage at a lower price), the movement from W to c_2 is inefficient since the perceived high-risk group lowers coverage.

Of course inaccurate classification may impose a constraint on the classification process. For example, if imperfect classification results in firms offering contract c_3 on $E_1L_1^P$ to the perceived low-risk group, firms will not participate in the classification process since the perceived low-risk group prefers the pooling contract W to contract c_3.

Figure 4.6 also illustrates an interesting case revealed in Hoy's work (49). If imperfect classification results in a very low proportion of low-risk individuals in the perceived high-risk group, as depicted by line EH^P, which lies to the left of the low-risk individuals indifference curve, U^L, then firms offer this group the separating equilibrium contract set (α^H, α^L) instead of a pooling contract.[5] Thus, under certain conditions, imperfect risk classification results in a pooling contract (c_1) for the perceived low-risk group and a separating contract (α^H, α^L) for the perceived high-risk group. Of course, all individuals in the perceived high-risk group

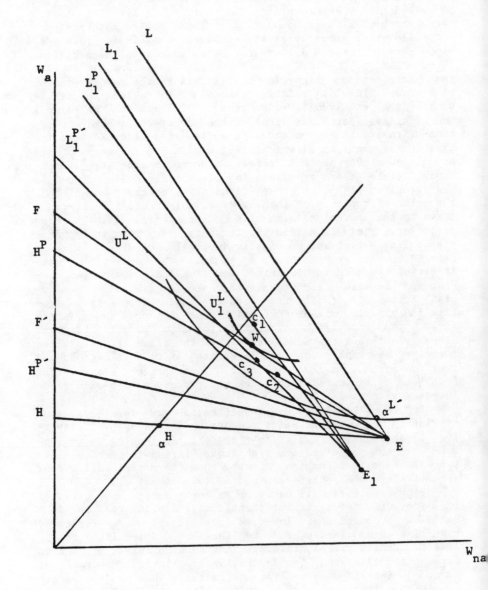

FIGURE 4.6

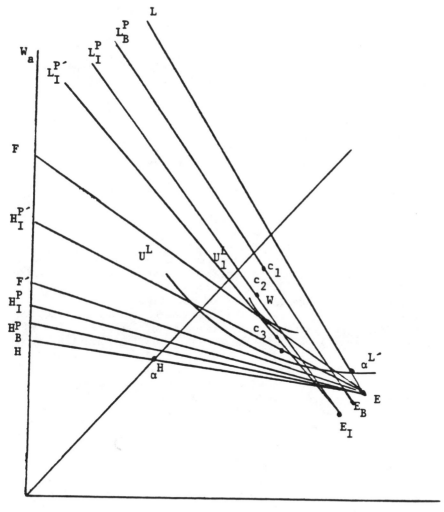

FIGURE 4.7

101

offered the separating contract $(\alpha^H, \alpha^{L'})$ are worse-off than the initial pooling equilibrium, W, before classification. Also notice that the occurrence of a separating equilibrium for the perceived high-risk group is dependent only on the accuracy of classification and not on its cost, since the cost, K, only affects the position of the perceived low-risk group's contract offer line. In addition, Figure 4.6 illustrates the effects of imperfect risk classification on market outcomes from an initial separating equilibrium. The market fair odds lines EF' is placed to the left of the low-risk individual's indifference curve U^L passing through point $\alpha^{L'}$ so that firms offer the separating contract $(\alpha^H, \alpha^{L'})$. Imperfect classification results in a contract line such as $E_1 L P_1$ offered to the perceived low-risk group and a contract line $EH^{P'}$ offered to the perceived high-risk group.[6] The market, then, offers the separating contract $(\alpha^H, \alpha^{L'})$ to the perceived high-risk group and the pooling contract c_1 to the perceived low-risk group. Thus, imperfect risk classification from an initial separating equilibrium is efficient since the perceived low-risk group is made better off and purchases more insurance (going from $(\alpha^H, \alpha^{L'})$ to c_1) and the perceived high-risk group remains the same purchasing contract $(\alpha^H, \alpha^{L'})$.

The possibility that the independent and bureau classification schemes differ in risk classification accuracy is now examined. For example, it might be the case that a rating bureau's classifications, based on the pooled experience of many firms, are more accurate than one firm's attempt at classifying risk. On the other hand, a large insurance firm with an adequate data base might have a better feel for classifying risks in its own markets and geographic regions. Both of these possibilities are considered in the diagrams below.

Figure 4.7 illustrates the case where bureau classification is more accurate than the independent scheme. Let the market fair odds line be EF such that a pooling equilibrium W is offered in the market. Bureau classification results in firms offering the contract c_1^P on line $E_B L_B$ to the perceived low-risk group and the separating contract $(\alpha^H, \alpha^{L'})$ to the perceived high-risk group whose fair odds line now is EH_B^P.[7] Notice that it is assumed that bureau classification is very accurate so that the perceived high-risk group contains a high proportion of high-risk individuals represented by the perceived high-risk p fair odds line EH_B which lies close to the actual high-risk fair odds line EH. Thus it is assumed bureau classification results in offering the perceived high-risk group a separating contract since line EH_B^P lies to the left of the low-risk individual's indifference curve U^L passing through point $\alpha^{L'}$.[8] The contract set $((\alpha^H, \alpha^{L'}), c_1)$ is an equilibrium set because any firm that offers the pooling W contract eventually incurs losses since the perceived low-risk group prefers c_1 to it.

It is now shown that independent classification, assumed less accurate than the bureau scheme, results in several possibilities. First, independent classification may be only slightly less accurate than the bureau scheme. In this case, independent classification results in firms offering the contract c_2 on line $E_I^L L_I$ to the perceived low-risk group and the separating contract $(\alpha^H, \alpha^{L'})$ to the perceived high-risk group whose fair odds line now is EH_I^P. Thus, when it is more accurate the bureau scheme clearly is superior (i.e., Pareto and efficient) to the independent scheme since the perceived low-risk group is better off and purchases more insurance at c_1 under the bureau scheme than purchasing contract c_2 under the independent scheme, while the perceived high-risk group purchases the separating contract $(\alpha^H, \alpha^{L'})$ under both schemes. Second, the independent scheme's inaccurate classification may be such that the line $EH_I^{P'}$ represents the perceived high-risk group's fair odds line. In this case, independent classification results in firms offering c_2 to the perceived low-risk group and contract c_3 to the perceived high-risk group. A comparison of bureau and independent classification is more difficult for this case. As previously stated, for the perceived low-risk group, c_1 under the bureau scheme is superior to c_2 under the independent scheme. However, the bureau scheme offers the separating contract $(\alpha^H, \alpha^{L'})$ to the perceived high-risk group while the independent scheme offers a pooling c_3 contract to the perceived high-risk group. Clearly, the independent scheme is a Pareto improvement over the bureau scheme since the perceived high-risk group prefers c_3 over $(\alpha^H, \alpha^{L'})$. An efficiency comparison between the pooling c_3 and the separating $(\alpha^H, \alpha^{L'})$ is difficult since neither is an efficient move from the initial pooling W contract. Thus, as this case shows, one cannot state unambiguously that the bureau scheme, even though less expensive and more accurate, is superior to the independent scheme since the perceived low-risk group is better off under the bureau scheme, while the perceived high-risk group is better off under the independent scheme. Surprisingly, then, less accurate classification, at least for the perceived high-risk group, may be desirable in that it might preclude the offering of separating contracts in favor of pooling contracts. And, finally, independent classification may result in the perceived low-risk contract offer line $E_I L_I^{P'}$ so that independent classification is economically unfeasible. Bureau classification obviously is superior in this case.

Figure 4.7 also illustrates a comparison of the bureau and independent schemes from an initial separating equilibrium. Assume, then, that the market fair odds line is EF' so that the contract set $(\alpha^H, \alpha^{L'})$ is initially offered in equilibrium. Under these conditions, the more accurate bureau classification, compared with the less accurate independent classification, is unambiguously superior to the independent scheme. To see this, recall that the bureau scheme results in the contract set $((\alpha^H, \alpha^{L'}), c_1)$ and the independent scheme results in the contract set $((\alpha^H, \alpha^{L'}), c_2)$. Thus the bureau scheme is superior since the perceived low-risk group prefers c_1 to c_2. Notice that inaccurate independent classification cannot result in firms offering pooling contracts (such as c_3 in the initial pooling W case) because the market fair odds line EF' now lies to the left of the low-risk group's indifference curve U^L passing through point $\alpha^{L'}$ so that the perceived high-risk fair odds line has to lie to the left of U^L since it must lie to the left of EF'. Thus from an initial separating equilibrium, a more accurate bureau scheme is always superior to a less accurate independent scheme.

Figure 4.8 illustrates the case where the bureau scheme is less accurate than the independent scheme. The independent scheme's accuracy advantage may or may not overcome the bureau scheme's cost advantage so that many cases are possible. Let us focus on the case where the independent scheme's accuracy advantage overcomes the bureau's cost advantage, for if it does not the outcomes are similar to the preceding analysis.

Let the market fair odds line be EF so that firms initially offer the equilibrium W contract. Bureau classification results in firms offering the contract c_1 on line $E_B L_B^P$ to the perceived low-risk group and the separating contract $(\alpha^H, \alpha^{L'})$, based on the perceived high-risk group's fair odds line, EH_B, to the perceived high-risk group. Independent classification, being more accurate than the bureau's classifications, results in firms offering contract c_2 on line $E_I L_I^P$ to the perceived low-risk group and the separating contract $(\alpha^H, \alpha^{L'})$ based on perceived high-risk group's fair odds line EH_I^P to the perceived high-risk group. In this case, then, independent classification is superior to bureau classification since the independent scheme's contract c_2 is a Pareto and efficient improvement over the bureau's c_1 contract, while both schemes offer the separating contract $(\alpha^H, \alpha^{L'})$ to the perceived high-risk group. However, there is the possibility that the bureau's accuracy is even less, so that line E_B^P' represents the perceived high-risk represents the perceived high-risk fair odds line. In this case the bureau scheme offers the pooling contract, c_3, to the perceived high-risk group instead the separating contract. Thus, a comparison of the two schemes is ambiguous since the perceived low-risk group is better off under the independent scheme, while the high-risk group is better off under the bureau scheme. Of course from an initial separating equilibrium firms can never offer pooling contracts to the perceived high-risk group,[9] so in this case the independent scheme always is superior to the bureau scheme.

In summation, the examinations of the bureau and independent classification schemes are revealing. If both schemes produce accurate classifications, their effects on market outcomes are efficient from both initial pooling and separating equilibriums with the bureau scheme superior to the independent

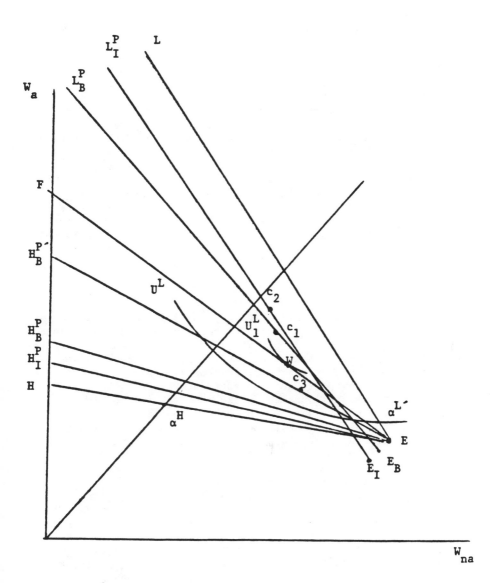

FIGURE 4.8

scheme. Also, independent classifications have a better chance
of surviving when the market offers separating contracts. However, if both schemes produce inaccurate classifications, a
comparison of the two schemes and their effects on market outcomes is not straightforward. For example, from initial pooling
equilibriums, inaccurate classification results in inefficient
outcomes, while from initial separating equilibriums, inaccurate classification results in efficient market outcomes. Also,
depending on the level of classification accuracy, the bureau
scheme may offer pooling contracts to the perceived high-risk
group while the independent scheme offers separating contracts
to the perceived high-risk group, or vice versa.   And that an
accurate independent scheme may overcome the bureau scheme's
cost advantage and produce more efficient market outcomes.
Finally, a comparison of the bureau and independent scheme's
effects on market outcomes (i.e., efficiency and Pareto
measurements) obviously depends on classification costs and
accuracies.   However, surprisingly, in some cases, the more
inaccurate the classification scheme the better chance it has
to compete with the more accurate scheme (this is the case when
accurate classification results in a separating contract for
the perceived high-risk group and inaccurate classification
results in a perceived high-risk pooled contract).

COMPETITIVE VERSUS REGULATED CLASSIFICATION

     Today's risk classification process is now examined more
closely by discussing how both competitive and regulated insurance environments deal with the risk classification process.
More specifically, the role rating bureaus and independent
firms play in the classification process are examined in both
regulated and competitive insurance markets.
     In today's insurance markets risk classification is
accomplished by firms employing rating bureau classifications,
firms independently classifying risks, or a combination of both
schemes, depending on the states' regulatory laws.   "In virtually all states, there are private rate bureaus that recommend
to their members a system for classifying and pricing risks.
The activities of the bureaus are subject to varying degrees of
oversight, depending on the state system of regulation and the
manner in which it is administered."[10] In the United States
approximately one-third of the states have adopted some form of
open competition laws and thus, two-thirds of the states have
remained in a regulatory climate.[11]   Several of the regulated
states, e.g., Louisiana, Mississippi, North Carolina, Texas,
and the District of Columbia, require rate bureau membership
as a condition for writing insurance.[12]   And in most regulated
states, the rating and classification systems are subject to
prior approval by state authorities.   In competitive insurance
states, such as California, New York, and Illinois, the

competitive climate has encouraged innovation in the form of coverage and rating classifications.[13] These innovations, in turn, lead to greater efficiency in the classification process. As suggested by MacAvoy (66): "Our own study of the California experience and the conclusions of the Stanford Research Institute suggest that the elimination of the artificial restraints on the risk assessment process and pricing mechanism would produce greater operating stability and predictability, which in turn may serve to minimize the (insurance) availability problem."[14] And the findings of the Stanford Research Institute study reports that there is "room for improvement in the risk assessment process" and the validity of some of the class relativities currently in use is questionable.[15]

The above discussion suggests that there are inefficiencies in the risk classification process and that a competitive insurance environment may improve it. Indeed, the independent pricing decisions of competing firms should aid the insurer in evaluating the relative efficiency of its risk classification system,[16] since price disseminates information about the insurance process. For example, the competitive insurance environment in California results in insurers differing in their selection and classification of drivers who may possess rating characteristics.[17] Thus, some insurance firms in California choose independently to classify risks and the accuracy of their classifications are enhanced by the independent price movements of competing insurers.[18]

The experience in Virginia also is a good example of a competitive insurance environment's effects on the risk classification process. Prior to 1974, Virginia had a prior approval system and thus any firm that desired a change in rules, rates, or rating plans had to get prior approval from the state insurance commission. Consequently, insurance firms in Virginia adhered to the rating bureau's (Insurance Services Office, ISO) rates and rating plans[19] which included only seven risk classes (or 9 classes if we include farmers). Virginia then adopted a competitive file-and-use insurance system (no prior approval of rating plan and rate changes were necessary) in 1974 and subsequently, on December 27, 1976, the state commission approved a 161 ISO risk class plan. Being in a competitive environment firms began independently to file their own risk plans with the insurance commission. Today approximately 75 firms have independently filed their own risk classifications.[20] And similar to California's experience with a competitive environment, Virginia's insurance industry since 1974 has exhibited loss ratios that are less volatile than regulated state's loss ratios.[21]

It may be inferred from the above discussion that a competitive insurance environment may exhibit risk classifications more accurate than those in a regulated insurance environment. Further, it appears that independent classifications are associated with a competitive environment and rating bureau class plans are associated with regulated environments. If competitive risk classification is more efficient than regulated risk classification then,[22] from a separating equilibrium, competitive classification is superior to regulated classification. That is, if the market initially offers separating contracts to a specific risk group, and firms want to further classify risk, it is better accomplished in a competitive environment than in a regulated environment. Both low-risk and high-risk groups are made better off in the competitive case.[23] However, the analyses also suggest that if the market initially offers pooling contracts a comparison of competitive and regulated risk classification process yields ambiguous results.

NOTES

1. MacAvoy (68), page 53.
2. For a complete review of the existence of separating and pooling equilibriums, see Chapter 3; the R-S-W model.
3. Hoy (49) was first to examine the effects of imperfect risk classification on market outcomes. However, his analysis is narrow in scope in that it neglects the different types of classification schemes and the cost of the classification process. Our analysis, then, is an extension of Hoy's. For a review of Hoy's work, see Chapter 2.
4. It also can be shown that the low-risk class bears the classification cost for imperfect classification. The graphical exposition, however, is quite tedious and will not be presented.
5. The feasibility of the existence of a separating equilibrium becomes possible when the market fair odds line i.e., $EH^{P'}$, lies to the left of the low risk individual's indifference curve, U^L, passing through point $\alpha^{L'}$, since a pooling contract offered on line EH^P represents lower utility for low-risk individuals.
6. Notice that the resulting perceived high-risk contract line EH^P has to lie to the left of the low-risk group's indifference curve U^L since the market fair odds line EF also lies to the left of U^L.
7. Notice that an intermediate step has been left out in the risk classification process. That is, a parallel shift of line EL to a line E_BL_B which reflects the cost of classification has been omitted to keep the diagram manageable.
8. The case where bureau classification is less accurate and consequently results in a pooling contract for the perceived high-risk group could have been easily examined. However, the aim is to compare bureau classification with less accurate independent classification so that the omission of the above case is appropriate.
9. The assertion that firms never offer pooling contracts to the perceived high-risk group from an initial separating equilibrium was demonstrated in the case where the bureau classification scheme was more accurate than independent classification.
10. MacAvoy (68), page 9.
11. National Association of Insurance Commissioners, staff study entitled "Monitoring Competition: A Means of Regulating the Property and Liability Insurance Business," 1974, pages 46-48.
12. Day (24), page 28.
13. New York Insurance Department Report (82), pp.114-21.
14. MacAvoy (68), page 40.
15. Stanford Research Institute Final Report (105), p.107.
16. MacAvoy (68), page 56.

17. Stanford Research Institute Final Report (105), pages
13-14.

18. MacAvoy (68) finds that at least 70 percent of the
insurance in California is priced independently of the bureau.
And the combination of independent pricing and independent risk
classification results in California firms exhibiting less
volatile loss ratios over a period of time (ten years) than
firms in the regulated states of New Jersey and Pennsylvania,
see MacAvoy (68), pages 25 and 26.

19. Virginia had two rating bureaus during this time
period: the Mutual Insurance Rating Bureau (MIRB) and the
National Bureau of Casualty Underwriters (NBCU). The MIRB
eventually folded and the NBCU later became known as the Insurance Services Office (ISO).

20. The number seventy-five was painstakingly arrived at
by physically counting the number of independent rating manuals
filed at the Virginia state corporation commission. I found
some firms submit classifications similar to the ISO class plan
while other firms submit class plans that markedly differ from
the ISO plan, e.g., Aetna Casualty and Surety company's class
plan involves 30 territories and 175 rating factors.

21. Virginia State Corporation Commission Report (111),
page 75. However, the data is far from conclusive since the
time period under study ends in 1977.

22. Notice it is assumed that the competitive market's
efficiency more than offsets the regulated (rating bureau) market's cost advantage of classifying risks.

23. See the preceding section for analysis.

5

Bank Insurance

INTRODUCTION

Similar to the accident insurance market, the bank insurance market also operates with information problems. Of course these information problems handicap insurance firms or banks in assessing properly the probabilities of bank failure. It is then important to assess the workings of the bank insurance market in the context of information problems.

The ensuing analysis recognizes that the main purpose of bank insurance is to insure depositors against loss from bank failure. And since transaction costs apparently prevent customers from purchasing deposit insurance individually, it is considered that banks are acting as agents for their customers in purchasing insurance for them. As Chapter 1 suggests, one reason it might be economical for the bank to serve as agent is that all customers of any one bank face the same probability of bank failure. Banks thus may aggregate customers' deposits and purchase insurance in their behalf, passing on premium costs in the prices they charge for services.

This chapter examines today's bank insurance market in the context of information problems. The first part examines a competitive bank insurance market. Specifically, R-S-W insurance model developed in Chapter 3 is adjusted to analyze competitive bank insurance market outcomes. A discussion on the existence of a competitive bank insurance market and the possibility of market breakdown is then offered. The chapter continues with examining the effects of the FDIC insurance arangement and its regulations on bank behavior. Specifically, the FDIC effects on bank behavior are divided into two parts: the effects on a

bank's liability management and the effects on a bank's asset
management.   And, finally, the possibility of classifying bank
risk is explored, resulting in a proposed alternative arrangement to the present FDIC insurance scheme.

COMPETITIVE BANK INSURANCE

This section examines a competitive bank insurance market.
The R-S-W model developed in Chapter 3, for a two-state, two-
risk group world is used except that now the market is for bank
insurance. For the bank insurance market there are two states:
failure (f) and no failure (nf).   Depositors (or banks acting
as their agents) participating in the insurance process are
assumed risk averse and they choose deposit coverage by maximizing their expected utility of deposit wealth. Firms which
are assumed to be risk neutral, offer insurance contracts based
on their maximizing expected profits. Further, assume for simplicity that there are only two types of banks in the market:
low-risk and high-risk banks with corresponding probabilities
of failure, p^L and p^H, where $p^L < p^H$. Initially, each risk group
is of the same size and faces the same loss, L.[1] Thus, the decision problems facing banks and insurance firms participating
in the bank insurance market are identical to the decision
problems individuals and insurance firms faced in Chapter 3
when participating in the accident insurance market. It follows
that the graphical expositions employed for accident insurance
are applicable for bank insurance.

Figure 5.1 below depicts a competitive bank insurance market, where the horizontal and vertical axes measure depositor
wealth in the failure state, W_{Df}, and no failure state, W_{Dnf},
respectively.   Assume both low-risk and high-risk banks start
with an initial endowment ($W_D - L$, W_D) at point E in an uninsured
state.   The sets of contracts offered by an insurance firm for
low-risk and high-risk banks which just break even are placed
in the diagram as lines EL and EH respectively.[2]   Indifference
curves are of the usual shape and are labeled U^L for the low-
risk group and U^H for the high-risk group.[3] If there is no information problem, so that firms can differentiate between low-
risk and high-risk banks and a competitive market exists, the
contract set (α^H, α^L) represents market equilibrium.   In other
words both low-risk and high-risk banks purchase full insurance
on their actuarially fair contract lines. This analysis implies
that if perfect information exists, firms will offer a number
of risk classes equal to the number of different probabilities
of bank failure. However, if firms are not able to differentiate between low-risk and high-risk banks, adverse selection may
result because high-risk banks will try to obtain contracts intended for low-risk banks. Recall that firms, in an attempt to
alleviate adverse selection, offer either separating contracts
or pooling contracts, depending on the composition of low-risk

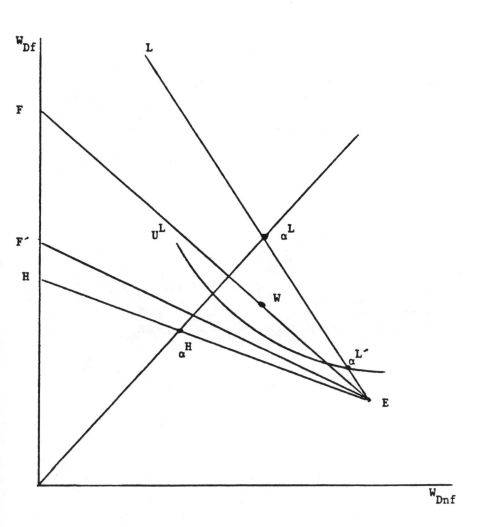

FIGURE 5.1

113

and high-risk banks in the market. Thus, if the market fair odds line is EF, the market offers the pooling equilibrium contract W and if the market fair odds line is EF´ the market offers the separating equilibrium contract set $(\alpha^H, \alpha^{L´})$.

It may be that in reality, banks have incomplete information about the probability they will fail. The probability not only depends on bank risk characteristics, such as its loan portfolio and captital outlays, but also on economic fluctuations which are beyond the control of individual banks.[4] For the same reasons insurance firms also can make only a limited assessment of the probability of bank failure.[5]

The model is now extended to accomodate incomplete information on the buyer (bank) side of the market. Incomplete information on the part of banks is represented by distinguishing between a bank's perceived probability of its own failure, p_*, and its actual probability of failure, p.[6] If a low-risk bank chooses an insurance policy based on the perceived low probability of failure, then of course its subjective expected utility, EV^L, is given by[7]

$$(1) \qquad EV^L_* = p^L_* U(W_D - L - \pi^L q + q) + (1 - p^L_*) U(W_D - \pi^L q).$$

Assuming the low-risk bank will maximize expected utility using perceived probabilities, first order conditions yield

$$(2) \qquad \frac{U´(W_D - L - (1 - \pi^L)q)}{U´(W_D - \pi^L q)} \frac{P^L_*}{1 - P^L_*} = \frac{\pi^L}{1 - \pi^L},$$

where the left-hand side of (2) represents the slope of a low-risk bank's subjective indifference curve and the right-hand side represents the slope of the budget line. Similarly, a high-risk bank's subjective expected utility EV^H_* and its first order conditions are given by

$$(3) \qquad EV^H_* = P^H_* U(W_D - L - \pi^H q + q) + (1 - P^H_*) U(W_D - \pi^H q) \qquad \text{and}$$

$$(4) \qquad \frac{U´(W_D - L - (1 - \pi^H)q)}{U´(W_D - \pi^H q)} \frac{P^H_*}{1 - P^H_*} = \frac{\pi^H}{1 - \pi^H}$$

respectively. Notice that the slopes of the subjective indifference curves (equations (2) and (4)) are affected by the direction of the misguided perceptions. For example, if low-risk banks misperceive their probabilities of failure so that P^L_* is less than P^L or P^L_* is greater than P^L, the slope of the subjective indifference curves, equation (2), will flatten or steepen relative to the curve based on correct probabilities.

Figure 5.2 below illustrates the effects of incomplete information from the buyer side on bank insurance market outcomes. Let us begin from the initial separating equilibrium $(\alpha^H, \alpha^{L´})$ so that the market fair odds line is EF´.[8] Consider the case where banks in the high-risk group underestimate their own probability of failure so that $P_*^H < P^H$. High-risk banks now desire to purchase a full coverage insurance policy on line EH´, depicted in Figure 5.2, with an associated price lower than the actuarially fair rate represented by the line EH. Line EH´ does not exist, however, since firms offering policies on this line would lose money. Thus high-risk banks will purchase less than full insurance on the contract offer line EH, since they perceive the price they pay to be greater than their perceived actuarially fair price.[9] The market then offers the separating contract set $(\alpha_1^H, \alpha^{L´´})$ to low-risk and high-risk banks. Contract α_1^H is purchased by high-risk banks since they desire partial coverage and low-risk banks are forced to insure partially at $\alpha^{L´´}$. Thus, low-risk banks have no real choice of insurance policy. The reason is adverse selection, which causes insurance firms to offer low-risk banks only the policies they offer high-risk banks. Low-risk banks' misperceptions about their probabilities of failure, then, have no effect on what separating policy they can purchase.

Since low-risk banks's misperceptions do affect the slope of their indifference curves, however, low-risk perceptions may force the market to switch from offering separating contracts to offering pooling contracts. To see this consider the case where the low-risk group underestimates its own probability of failure so that $P_*^L < P^L$ which results in a flat U_1^L low-risk subsubjective indifference curve. Notice that the separating offering $(\alpha_1^H, \alpha^{L´´})$ is no longer an equilibrium. A firm can offer the pooling W contract and earn non-negative profits, since the low-risk group prefers W to $\alpha^{L´´}$. Hence, in this case, consumer misperception about risk (bank failure) may force the market to switch from offering separating contracts to offering pooling contracts. On the other hand, the market may continue to offer the separating contract $(\alpha_1^H, \alpha^{L´´})$ if low-risk banks overestimate their own probabilities of failure. In this case, $P_*^L > P^L$ results in the U_2^L subjective indifference curve which lies to the right of the market fair odds line EF´ and thus the separating contract set $(\alpha_1^H, \alpha^{L´´})$ is an equilibrium.

Now consider the case where high-risk banks overestimate their own probabilities of failure so that $P_*^H > P^H$. High-risk banks will initially desire full coverage on their perceived actuarially fair contract line EH´´ in Figure 5.2. Firms offering contracts on line EH´´ to high-risk banks would make positive profits, however, so entry by other firms would ensue to force price to the actuarially fair level on contract line EH. Thus, in this case, high-risk banks would fully insure at α^H. The market then offers the contract set $(\alpha^H, \alpha^{L´´})$. And, again depending on the low-risk banks' perceived probabilities of failure, in equilibrium the market will offer either the separating contract $(\alpha^H, \alpha^{L´})$ or the pooling contract, W.

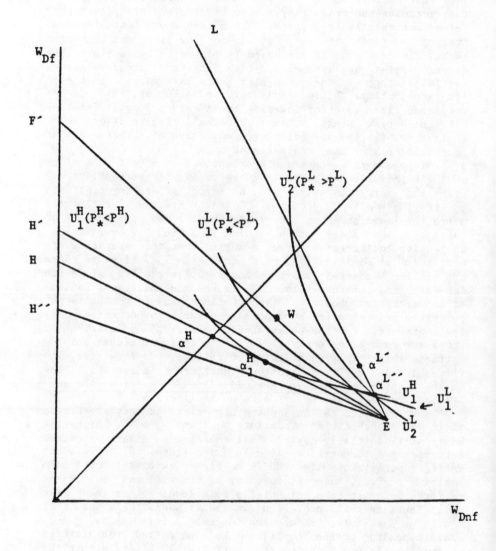

FIGURE 5.2

116

Thus far, the analysis suggests that bank misperceptions may lead to undesirable market outcomes from initial separating equilibriums. For example, if high-risk banks underestimate probabilities of failure, the resulting market equilibrium is not a Pareto outcome. High-risk banks are found to purchase less insurance (moving from α_1^H to α^H) and low-risk banks also purchase less insurance (moving from α to $\alpha^{L'}$). And even if pooling contracts result, the move is not Pareto since the low-risk banks prefer $\alpha^{L'}$ (in the $P_*^L = P$ case) to W. Finally, for the case where the high-risk bank overestimates its own probability of failure, if a separating contract is offered it is identical to the initial separating arrangement, and if a pooling contract is offered, both risk groups remain at W.

Figure 5.3 illustrates the effects of incomplete information on the buyer side from an initial pooling equilibrium. The market fair-odds line is EF so that the market initially offers the pooling contract W in equilibrium. To aid in the examination (from a pooling equilibrium) take note of the fact that the position of a pooling contract is determined by the low-risk group.[10] Thus, the direction of a low-risk bank's misguided perception determines the position of the pooling contract for both low-risk and high-risk banks in the market.

For example, consider the case where low-risk banks underestimate their probabilities of failure so that $P_*^L < P^L$. Low-risk banks now perceive the price of the pooling contract W reflected by line EF to be higher than when low-risk banks with perfect perceptions (i.e., $P_*^L < P^L$) purchased contract W. Thus, low-risk banks reduce coverage from contract W if $P_*^L < P^L$. The market then offers the pooling contract W_1 in equilibrium. Similarly, if $P_*^L > P^L$, low-risk banks desire more coverage and consequently the market offers the pooling contract W_2 in equilibrium. Bank misperceptions from an initial pooling equilibrium either reduce or increase coverage, depending on the direction of the misguided low-risk bank's perception of bank failure. The high-risk bank's misperception has no effect on pooling contracts.

Of course in a bank insurance market where both insurance firms and banks have incomplete information about banks' probabilities of failure many different market outcomes are possible. The above examination serves to explain how these market outcomes may come about. In actuality there are eight possible cases of banks misperceptions about their own bank failures.[11] And coupled with the inabilities of insurance firms to differentiate among banks' risks and the market composition of low-risk and high-risk banks in the market, a myriad of market outcomes is possible.

While some high-risk banks underestimate their probabilities of failure, $P_*^H < P^H$, some other high-risk banks may overestimate their probabilities of failure, $P_*^H > P^H$. Similarly, it is possible for low-risk banks to be divided into a $P_*^L < P^L$ group and a $P_*^L > P^L$ group. Differing perceptions of failure within

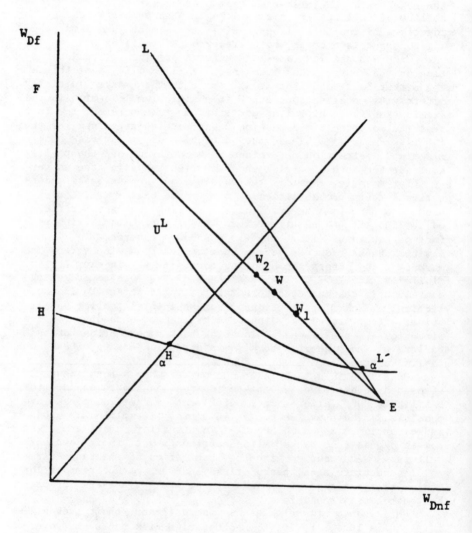

FIGURE 5.3

118

bank risk groups also may generate multiple equilibria contract offerings. A competitive bank insurance market with a dual information problem (i.e., both seller and buyer have incomplete information about bank failure), then, can be characterized by the offering of multiple equilibria contract offerings reflecting the many different possible market outcomes. And generally these outcomes are not optimal in a Pareto sense.

MARKET FAILURE

To see how a bank insurance market's information problems may lead to market failure, consider the following scenario.[12] Suppose there are n insurance firms and two types of banks, low-risk and high-risk banks, participating in a bank insurance market. Assume both firms and banks have information problems. Firms are unable to differentiate between low-risk and high-risk banks and banks do not have accurate assessments of their own probabilities of failure. Assume further that firms also have difficulty assessing the probabilities (low- and high-risks) of bank failure. Thus, in our diagrams (i.e., Figures 5.2 and 5.3) the separating and pooling contracts offered by firms, in their attempts to alleviate adverse selection, may be based on inaccurate assessments of bank failure. In other words, the contract lines EL and EH for separating contracts and EF for pooling contracts may not accurately represent the true odds line of the risk group is question. Changing economic conditions, poor management, and poor investments are all factors that may determine the position of the contract lines. These factors are beyond the control of banks and thus beyond the abilities of insurance firms to use in accurately assessing bank risk.

It follows, then, that there may be some degree of instability in insurance firms' operations. For example, if firms underestimate bank risk then the true claims made on insurance firms are greater than the premiums paid in, which results in firm losses. This in turn implies that there is some positive probability p^S that firms will be unable to pay off claims. Suppose banks cannot differentiate among insurance firms' probabilities of insolvencies, p^S, so that banks use insurance premiums as the only criterion for purchasing insurance. Banks then choose insurance firms offering the lowest premiums, and assuming all other things equal the lower the premium the higher the probability of insolvency. Thus, high-risk insurance firms (i.e., they have high probabilities, p^S, of insolvency) eventually drive out low-risk insurance firms. And as the high-risk insurance firms come to dominate the market, banks purchase less and less insurance since they observe more and more insolvencies. Hence, the bank insurance market inevitably fails.

FDIC DEPOSIT INSURANCE

The previous sections demonstrate that severe information problems in the bank insurance process may preclude a well functioning competitive bank insurance market and, thus, they can provide a rationale for government intervention.   Indeed, without a formal bank insurance market to insure bank deposits, more than a third of the nation's banks failed during the 1920s.   The vulnerability of the banking system during the years of the Great Depression suggested a need for a formal bank insurance market to help assure soundness in the banking structure.   One attempt to satisfy this need was the Banking Act of 1933, which led to the creation of the Federal Deposit Insurance Corporation (FDIC).   The FDIC was established to restore public confidence in the banking system, to protect de-positors from deposit loss due to bank failure, and to promote safe and sound banking practices.   The FDIC pursues these purposes today through a program of deposit insurance coverage and through the regulation and supervision of its member banks not subject to the Federal Reserve's supervisory control.

In providing deposit insurance to banks, the FDIC sets premiums at a uniform rate based on the bank's total deposits rather than its insured deposits.   In many cases the premium probably is not actuarially fair, because the premium rate does not vary with each bank's probability of failure.   At present, the FDIC insures depositors of its member banks to a maximum of $100,000.

Let us now examine FDIC deposit insurance in the bank insurance model.   It is recognized that the FDIC is a monopoly since it is the only seller of bank insurance.   It is also recognized that insurance premiums are not based on bank risk or coverage desired, but on total deposits.   The insurance premium, kD, denotes the amount of FDIC charged all banks for insurance, where k is the charge per dollar of deposits, D.

Figure 5.4 illustrates the effects of FDIC deposit insur-ance on market outcomes.   Assume low-risk and high-risk banks exist and they start with an initial endowment (W_D-L, W_D) at point E in an uninsured state.   Thus no distinction is made be-tween small and big depositors. All customers initially deposit the same amount of dollars in low-risk and high-risk banks.[13] Further assume that this deposit dollar amount must not exceed $100,000 so that FDIC deposit insurance fully insures every bank customer.   Low-risk and high-risk banks are assumed to be the same size in that they possess the same dollar amount of total deposits. This assumption implies that low-risk and high-risk banks pay the same FDIC insurance premium for bank insur-ance, where the low-risk bank premium, kD^L, is equal to the high-risk bank premium, kD^H.[14] Thus, low-risk and high-risk banks take out full deposit coverage for their customers by purchasing a pooling FDIC insurance contract at a price of kD dollars. It follows that the price of insurance, kD ($=kD^L=kD^H$) must closely reflect the market fair odds line, EF (in Figure 5.4) for the low-and high-risk banks in the market. Indeed, this is true in the long-run, for if it were false we should expect the FDIC to earn abnormally high profits or incur significant losses over a period of time. For deposit insurance the FDIC charges participating banks one twelfth of one percent of their total deposits annually. The charges are returned to the institutions, less any losses paid out.[15] It is fair then to assume that, in general, the FDIC offers an actuarially fair priced pooling contract. Hence, in Figure 5.4, both low- and high-risk banks purchase the pooling contract, c_1, on the market fair odds line EF.

These findings reveal a marked contrast between a competitive bank insurance market's outcomes and an FDIC bank insurance market's outcomes. For example, if in a competitive market as depicted in Figure 5.4, the market fair odds line is EF such that firms offer a pooling W contract, FDIC deposit insurance makes low-risk banks worse off since low-risk benefits are maximized at point W on line EF (i.e., U^L lies above U_1^L), while high-risk banks are made better off purchasing more desired coverage (going from W to c_1). And if the market fair odds line is EF´ such that firms offer the separating contracts ($\alpha^H, \alpha^{L´}$), FDIC deposit insurance again makes low-risk banks worse off (going from $\alpha^{L´}$ to c_2) while the high-risk banks are made better off (going from α^H to c_2). Thus, in a competitive insurance environment, FDIC insurance results in non-Pareto market outcomes.

Of course a competitive bank insurance market with symmetric information problems (i.e., both firms and banks have difficulty assessing failure probabilities) may exhibit many possible non-Pareto market outcomes and thus FDIC insurance may serve to improve market outcomes. Further, as an earlier section indicated, a competitive bank insurance market's information problems may lead to market failure, making the presence of FDIC insurance even more valuable to society. This discussion then suggests that the FDIC deposit insurance arrangement is a second-best solution in that it is an improvement over an insurance market with symmetric information problems, but falls short on resolving how a bank insurance market most effectively might deal with the information problems. Moreover, the FDIC insurance arrangement precludes risk classification. No effort is made to improve market outcomes by classifying banks according to risk.

Let us now relax the assumption that all customers possess identical deposits which do not exceed $100,000. In other words, allow customers to differ in their deposits where some customers deposit $100,000 or less and some customers deposit more than $100,000. In effect, the merits of FDIC assessments of insurance premiums based on total deposits rather than on insured deposits are now examined.

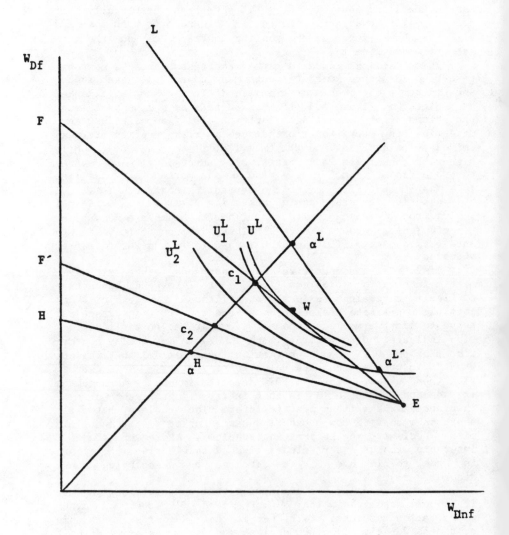

FIGURE 5.4

122

Figure 5.5 illustrates how the FDIC insurance arrangement affects market outcomes in the bank insurance market model. Suppose there are two types of depositors, small and big depositors, belonging to both low-and high-risk banks, where small depositors initially deposit, D_S = \$100,000 and big depositors initially deposit, D_B = \$150,000. Figure 5.5 depicts the initial endowment points for small and big depositors as E_S and E_B respectively. Endowment points E_S and E_B are on the horizontal axis because if banks fail, depositors lose all of their deposits. Let lines $E_S L_S$ and $E_B L_B$ represent the fair odds lines for small and big depositors belonging to low-risk banks. Notice that lines $E_S L_S$ and $E_B L_B$ are parallel since small and big depositors belonging to low-risk banks face the same probability of failure. Similarly, lines $E_S H_S$ and $E_B H_B$ represent the fair odds lines for small and big depositors belonging to high-risk banks. If the FDIC offers a pooling contract to low- and high-risk banks where small and big depositors pay the same price and are both allowed to insure fully, contracts c_S and c_B are purchased by small and big depositors respectively. [16] That is, small depositors purchase contract c_S on the market fair odds line $E_S F_S$ and big depositors purchase contract c_B on their market fair odds line $E_B F_B$. And assuming, for simplicity, that there is an equal number of small and big depositors in low-risk and high-risk banks, the market fair odds lines $E_S F_S$ and $E_B F_B$ are parallel and thus small and big depositors pay the same price for insurance.

However, in actuality, big depositors cannot fully insure since FDIC insurance coverage is to \$100,000 while big depositors have \$150,000 in deposits. Thus, big depositors not only partially insure but they end up paying more for insurance than small depositors. To see this, recall that FDIC premiums are based on total deposits and not insured deposits. Insurance premiums paid by small depositors, kD_S, then are less than premiums paid by big depositors, kD_B (since coverage is for \$100,000 for both small and big depositors). In Figure 5.5, big depositors pay a price kD_B that is greater than the actuarially fair pooled price (reflected by line $E_B F_B$). If line line $E_B'F_B$ represents such a line, big depositors now purchase contract c_B' since they also are forced to partially insure. It also follows that small depositors purchase full FDIC coverage for a price that is less than their actuarially fair odds line $E_S F_S$ since the overall FDIC insurance premium for the entire market is assumed to be actuarially fair. [17] If line $E_S F_S$ reflects this reduced price, then small depositors fully insure by purchasing contract c_S' on line $E_S'F_S'$. Hence, the present FDIC insurance arrangement results in big depositors partially insuring by purchasing a high-priced c_B' pooling contract, while small depositors fully insure by purchasing a low-priced c_S' pooling contract.

Big depositors not only are ineligible for complete insurance protection, but they actually subsidize small depositors.

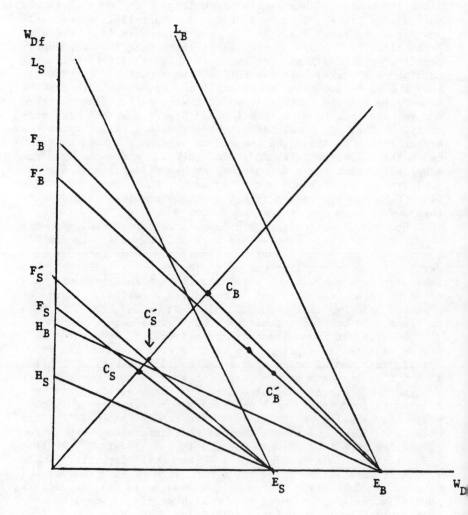

FIGURE 5.5

In Figure 5.5 the subsidy can be measured by the change in the
slope reflected by the rotation of line E_BF_B to line E_BF_B'. It
It follows then that the amount of the subsidy also depends on
the composition of small and big depositors in low-risk and
high-risk banks since this composition affects the relative
slopes of E_BF_B and E_SF_S.

The above FDIC deposit insurance arrangement resulting in
big depositors partially insuring and subsidizing small depositors obviously is not an equitable arrangement. However,
in a competitive insurance environment with asymmetric information (a benchmark used throughout the examinations) it is
possible that all depositors will partially insure. For
example, if a pooling contract is offered in a competitive
environment all depositors partially insure since firms maximize low-risk banks, benefits. Low-risk banks prefer partial
coverage when faced with a price greater than their expected
costs. And if a separating contract is offered, low-risk banks
partially insure while high-risk banks fully insure. Hence, a
market free from FDIC intervention cannot be expected to always
offer full coverage contracts. An alternative FDIC arrangement
may be necessary to improve equity and efficiency for bank
insurance.

FDIC EFFECTS ON BANK BEHAVIOR

FDIC insurance arrangements not only affect the bank
insurance process, but also bank behavior. Thus, to assess
fairly the FDIC process, the effects of the FDIC insurance
scheme and its regulations on bank behavior must also be examined. This section divides the effects of the FDIC arrangement
into two distinct parts: the effects on a bank's liability
management and the effects on a bank's asset management. On
the liability side an analysis of how the FDIC insurance premium affects a bank's desired deposits is offered. Also, the
effects of interest rate restrictions (such as regulation Q, a
maximum interest rate that banks may pay on saving deposits) on
bank behavior are examined. Recently rate restrictions are
being phased out (via the Depository Monetary Control Act of
1980) and are now less imposing on bank behavior. However,
restrictions still do exist and an examination will prove useful. On the asset side, the effects of FDIC restrictions on
the assets a bank can hold are discussed. Also an analysis of
how the FDIC insurance premium affects a bank's risk position
on the efficient portfolio frontier is offered.

Bank Liability Management

Since the FDIC sets premiums based on total deposits, and
not on banks' risk, insurance premiums may affect the amount of

deposits banks desire.   This effect can easily be demonstrated by adding the deposit premium to a bank's objective function.

Let us suppose that a bank maximizes a simple profit function where revenues and costs are derived solely from its loans and demand deposits.[18]   Denote the term $R_L L$ as total revenue, where R_L is the rate of return on loans, L, the bank charges to all customers.   Also denote total cost by the term $R_D D$ where R_D is the rate of return which the bank pays to all customers on demand deposits, D.   Now let the term kD denote the amount the FDIC charges all banks for insurance, where k is the charge per dollar of deposits.   If we let Φ represent profits, the bank's maximization problem becomes

$$(5) \qquad \max \Phi = R_L L - R_D D - kD.$$

Let us further assume that the supply of demand deposits to the individual bank is an increasing function of its yield so that

$$(6) \qquad D = D(R_D)$$

and that the amount of funds allocated to bank loans is a fraction, X, of demand deposits, so that[19]

$$(7) \qquad L = XD.$$

The bank's maximization problem now becomes

$$(8) \qquad \max \Phi = XR_L D(R_D) - R_D D(R_D) - k_D(R_D).$$

Differentiating with respect to the rate of return on deposits and setting the result equal to zero for a maximum yields

$$(9) \qquad \frac{\partial \Phi}{\partial R_D} = XR_L D'(R_D) - R_D D'(R_D) - D(R_D) - k_D' (R_D) = 0.$$

Solving for $D(R_D)$ results in

$$(10) \qquad D^*(R_D) = XR_L D'(R_D) - R_D D'(R_D) - kD'(R_D).$$

Condition (10) tells us that the amount of deposits a bank desires, D^*, is lowered by the marginal effect an increase in deposits has on the cost of insurance, $kD'(R_D)$.   Purchasing insurance may thus affect the bank's liability management.   This should be intuitively clear since the insurance premium is based on the bank's liabilities.   Of course banks will pass the cost of insurance,   kD,   on to its customers through higher prices for services, where a lower interest rate paid to customers for deposits indicates higher priced services.

Deposit premiums can thus affect liability management. However, a bank's riskiness derives from asset management policy.   Since insurance premiums do not directly affect a bank's asset portfolio, premiums are not sensitive to bank riskiness. An interest rate restriction such as regulation Q, however, is an attempt to reduce banks' probability of failure on the liability side. This particular regulation gives authority to the Federal Reserve to set the maximum interest rate that commercial banks may pay on time deposits. The FDIC has the same authority over nonmember's so that Regulation Q applies to almost all banks. As stated earlier, rate restrictions are being phased out, but some still do exist. The original purpose of Regulation Q was strikingly similar to the reasons given for insurance rate regulation in the accident insurance market delineated in Chapter 3: to limit price competition so as to allay solvency problems caused by price wars. As with accident insurance firms, banks also possess a large part of society's wealth, so that any one bank's failure would have an adverse impact on a significant segment of the economy. And in another similarity with accident insurance, the remedy for problems of the banking market was partly by anti-competitive measures, namely regulating price.

Two problems, however, are associated with interest rate restrictions that aggravate instead of allay the soundness of the bank system. First, rate regulation (such as Regulation Q) induces an inefficiency with respect to the allocation of financial resources. Consider the savings market depicted in Figure 5.6 below. The market clearing interest rate, r_m, is associated with an amount of funds, S_m, deposited in banks. If the interest rate allowed under Regulation Q is a binding constraint for banks, an excess demand for funds will result. Banks will demand S_2 amount of funds, but customers are willing to supply only S_1. Thus $S_M - S_1$ represents the loss of savings due to Regulation Q. This distortion is aggravated when banks attempt to reduce the $S_2 - S_1$ gap. Inducements such as gifts, special services, and advertisements are examples of devices banks use in competing for funds. Also, banks have created other financial instruments, such as certificates of deposits, in order to circumvent Regulation Q. Hence, regulating the price of funds elicits bank behavior which would not otherwise have existed under a competitive regime. The second problem arises from the effect of high inflation on interest rates. Since the interest rate on time deposits is regulated, and a high anticipated rate of inflation raises nominal interest rates, time deposits may not be able to compete with instruments such as treasury bills or commercial paper in a time of inflation. Inflation may force a decrease in the volume of bank funds and can inhibit bank competitiveness in the financial market.[20]

The costs of interest rate regulation appear to be substantial. The rationale behind rate restrictions is to inhibit price competition and thus promote stability in the bank market. However, regulating interest rates does not inhibit price competition. Banks circumvent price regulations by creating

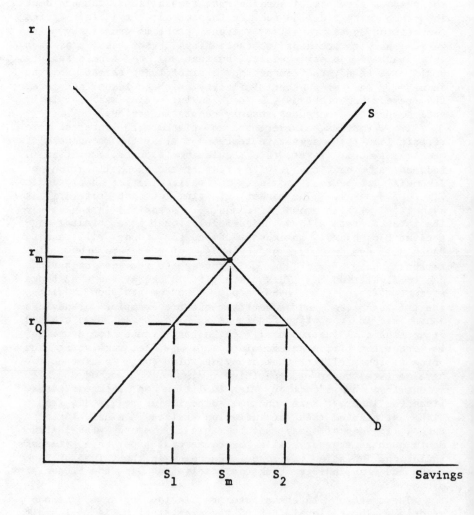

FIGURE 5.6

128

new financial instruments and compete in their prices. Also, price regulation increases non-price competition. Hence, it appears that this type of regulation aggravates market outcomes instead of allaying market problems.

Bank Asset Management

As previously stated, a bank's riskiness derives from asset management policy and thus regulating bank assets provides a more direct link with bank riskiness. The Federal Reserve and the FDIC do impose asset restrictions as an attempt to control bank riskiness. However, these restrictions may in fact promote excessive risk taking. For example, some FDIC restrictions limit the quantity of funds a bank may allocate to a single asset, thus limiting the amount of capital exposed to any one borrower. Koehn (61) demonstrates that this type of restriction will alter the efficient portfolio frontier, making bank portfolios riskier. His anlaysis was discussed in Chapter 2. The conclusions he reached are that asset restrictions may increase the risk of each portfolio for a given rate of return. This means asset restrictions may have the perverse effect of making banks engage in riskier activities.

The effects of the FDIC premium arrangement on bank asset management are now examined. Consider a bank where there exists no regulation and no formal bank insurance. Assume banks are profit maximizing firms engaged in the business of banking; they borrow money from the public and in return provide a checking service or interest payment and they lend this money to firms at a higher interest charge, or they invest in bonds at a higher interest rate. The differential in interest rates, and amounts borrowed and invested, determine their profits. Let us suppose that all deposits, D, borrowed at interest rate, R_D, are available to the banks' investment portfolios. Thus any deposit issued by a bank goes directly to its investment portfolio which consists of bonds and loans to business firms. Given the interest rate banks pay depositors, R_D, and the appropriate rates of return and risk associated with various investment opportunities, banks will choose an investment portfolio consistent with their tastes. This situation is illustrated formally with the use of Figures 5.7 and 5.8 below. The horizontal axis measures the risk associated with each investment portfolio. The standard deviation of portfolio return, σ_p, is used as this proxy. The vertical axis measures the expected return on each portfolio, $E(R_p)$. Thus any point in expected return, risk space represents a bank portfolio consisting of bonds and loans.

Let us assume banks are rational investors and choose to hold efficient portfolios. A portfolio is efficient if it maximizes expected returns for a given degree risk or, what is the same thing, if it minimizes risk for a given expected

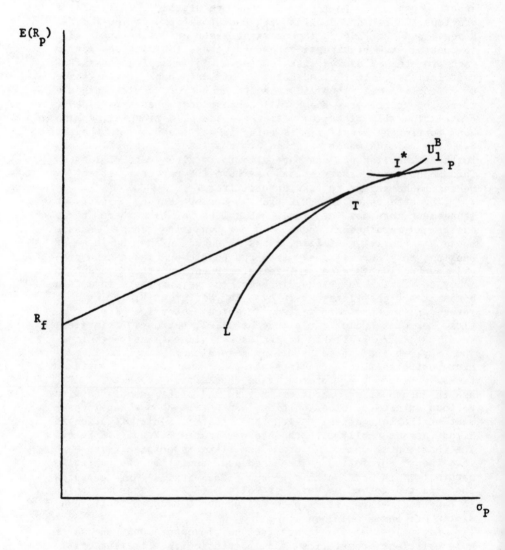

FIGURE 5.7

130

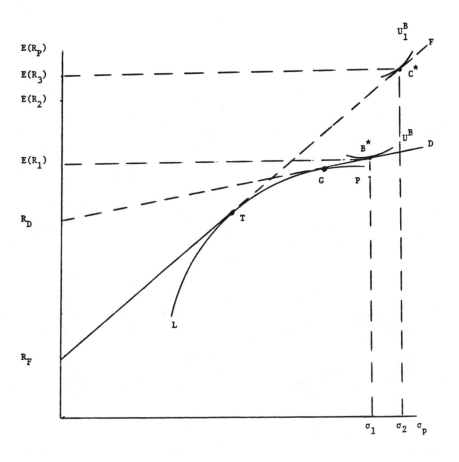

FIGURE 5.8

131

return.[21]   The efficient portfolio frontier faced by a bank is represented by curve LP in Figure 5.7.   If borrowing is not permitted, the bank will choose a point on LP based on its utility function.   Such a choice is depicted by the tangency of a bank's indifference curve (derived from its utility function) U_1^B, on the efficient frontier, LP.   The bank will then choose I^* as its investment portfolio.[22]   However, if a riskless asset is available at interest rate, R_f, the bank's efficient frontier can be constructed by a line drawn from R_f to a point of tangency, T, on frontier LP.   Thus the segment R_fTP now becomes the efficient frontier for all banks.   Consequently, a bank's investment portfolio is determined by the tangency of its indifference curve to a point on line R_fTP.

If banks are allowed to issue deposits (borrow) the efficient frontier is altered.   This situation is illustrated in Figure 5.8, which contains the efficient frontier LP. Denote R_f as the riskless asset so that any point on R_fT represents identical portfolios differing only in the proportion of funds allocated between the riskless asset and all other assets. Let R_D represent the interest rate banks pay depositors for use of their money. It is important to notice that R_D is placed above R_f in Figure 5.8.   The interest rate paid on deposits must be greater than the interest rate paid on a riskless asset because there is a risk associated with a bank's ability to pay depositors in case of failure.   Since deposits are not insured in case of bank failure, depositors demand a higher return on their money (a risk premium) for bearing uncertainty.[23]

A bank may now issue deposits at R_D and allocate these funds to its investment portfolio. The situation is represented by drawing a line from R_D tangent to LP at some point G and extended out to point D.   The solid portion of this line, GD, represents borrowing.   The efficient portfolio frontier now is composed of three sections.   Lending occurs on segment R_fT, borrowing occurs on segment GD and there are efficient portfolios between T and G.   Notice that since R_D is greater than R_f the line R_DD is flatter than R_fT.   Recalling that a bank is in business to borrow money in a form of deposits and transfer these funds to its investment portfolio, a bank will choose a point on the segment GD based on its utility function.   Let us represent such a choice by the tangency of a bank's indifference curve, U^B, on the segment, GD.   The bank then chooses B^* as its investment portfolio with an associated expected return $E(R_1)$ and risk σ_1, on its investments. Hence, the return, risk combination, $E(R_1)$, σ_1, established by B^*, defines the bank's risk position in the market.

Let us now consider a bank market where there is no regulation like Regulation Q or any asset restriction, but a formal insurance market controlled by the FDIC does exist. Recall the FDIC sets premiums based on total deposits.   As of 1980 the FDIC insured deposits up to $100,000.   For simplicity, assume $100,000 is full coverage for all customers.[24]   Customers view all banks as possessing the same degree of risk, since their deposits now are insured. And since their investments are insured by a government backed FDIC, the risk of deposits are commensurate with the riskless government-backed assets. Hence, depositors no longer demand a risk premium for loaning their money and are satisfied with the riskless rate of return, R_f.[25] This situation is depicted in Figure 5.8 where, in our FDIC world, banks borrow deposits at the riskless rate, R_f. It follows that banks now establish their portfolios on the segment TF for similar reasons that banks possessed portfolios on segment GD in the no-insurance world. Given that banks' utility functions are identical in both the non-insured and insured worlds, an important question is where the point of tangency between the banks' indifference curves and segment TF lies. If they lie to the left of portfolio B^*, FDIC insurance induces banks to take less risky positions. And if the new portfolio lies directly above portfolio B^*, FDIC insurance has no effect on bank risk positions. However, if the new portfolio lies to the right of portfolio B^*, FDIC insurance indirectly induces banks to take riskier positions in the market.

Notice that FDIC insurance rotates segment GD counter-clockwise to TF. As Figure 5.8 depicts, this means that for a given risk, σ_1, banks receive a higher return on their portfolios where $E(R_2)$ is greater than $E(R_1)$. The slopes of segments GD and TF are the prices of risk avoidance, and with FDIC insurance that price has decreased. It is useful then to interpret the movement from GD to TF as the change in the price of the investment portfolio, B^*. The price has decreased, which leads to subsequent substitution and income effects. Of course the impact of these effects depends on the particular utility functions employed. The utility functions most widely used in portfolio literature (which best depict reality) are two parameter functions such as the logarithmic, power, and exponential. All three of these utility functions exhibit constant relative risk aversion, which implies an income effect of zero and thus a substitution effect that dominates. For example, consider the logarithmic utility function,

(11) $$E(\log(1+\tilde{R}_p))$$

where $\tilde{R}_p$ is the rate of return on the portfolio. Let μ and σ^2 represent the mean and variance of $\tilde{R}_p$. Thus if we approximate (11), it becomes[26]

(12) $$\mu - \frac{\sigma^2}{2}.$$

The slope of the indifference curve from (12) can be derived by taking the total differential and setting the result equal to zero. Thus,

$$(13) \qquad \frac{\partial \mu}{\partial \mu} \, d\mu + \frac{\partial \mu}{\partial \sigma} \, d\sigma - \sigma d\sigma - \sigma \, \frac{\partial \sigma}{\partial \mu} \, d\mu = 0.$$

Simplifying (13), results in

$$(14) \qquad \frac{d\mu}{d\sigma} = \sigma.$$

Equation (14) is then differentiated by μ, since it tells us how a change in μ affects the slope of the indifference curve holding σ constant. This results in

$$(15) \qquad \frac{\partial}{\partial \mu} \left| \frac{d\mu}{d\sigma} \right|_{\sigma = constant} = 0$$

Thus for a change in expected return, μ, the slope of the indifference curve does not change. It follows that the income effect is zero. Hence, for this class of utility functions, the substitution effect always dominates over the income effect. It follows that the tangency of the bank's indifference curve to TF lies to the right of portfolio B^*. Banks then purchase a portfolio C^* depicted in Figure 5.8. Hence, the new risk, return combination, $E(R_3)$, σ_2, established by portfolio C^* possesses a greater return, risk combination than the return risk combination, $E(R_1)$ σ_1, established by portfolio B^*. Thus, FDIC insurance indirectly induces banks to take riskier positions in the market.

Introducing interest rate regulation into the above model is easily accomplished.[27] Three cases are possible. First, if the rate restriction, R_Q, is not binding, i.e., R_Q is greater than R_D, the results just described are duplicated. When the rate restrict is binding there is a second case where $R_f < R_Q < R_D$ and a third case where $R_Q < R_f$. These last two cases alter the above results. These cases are illustrated in Figure 5.9 below. Figure 5.9 duplicates Figure 5.8 in that lines $R_D GD$ and $R_f TF$ and frontier LP are presented. For the second and third cases the rate restriction is denoted as R_Q^2 and R_Q^3 respectively.

If $R_f < R_Q^2 R_D$, the segment WQ_2 becomes the relevant portion of the efficient portfolio frontier for banks. Thus for reasons presented in the analysis above, banks will choose portfolio E^*. In this case, two effects are possible as a result of a rate restriction. First, the rate restriction does not affect a bank's risk position in an environment with FDIC insurance, since R_Q^2 is not binding when R_f is the riskless rate on deposits. Second, the rate restriction does affect a bank's risk position in a no-insurance environment, since R_Q^2 is binding when R_D is the rate on deposits. In this case banks' portfolios change from B^* to E^* and, as evident in Figure 5.8, their risk positions subsequently increase.

If $R_Q^3 < R_f$, the segment VQ_3 becomes the relevant portion of the efficient portfolio frontier for banks, and banks invest in

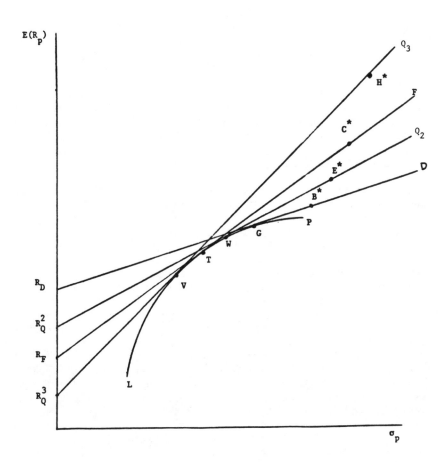

FIGURE 5.9

portfolio H^*. As Figure 5.9 clearly depicts, the regulation Q_3 ceiling increases a bank's risk position in both a non-FDIC and FDIC environment, where B^* increases to E^* and C^* increases to H^* respectively.

One final note concerning this analysis. If the explicit payment of insurance premiums by bank customers via lower interest payments paid to customers on their deposits is considered, the directions of the results of the above analysis do not change; only the magnitudes change.   In other words, banks pass on the cost of insurance by lowering the interest rate paid on deposits, which is the cost of bank borrowing. And thus the price of risk banks face decreases (the slopes of the appropriate segments in Figure 5.9 steepens) which induces banks to take riskier positions in the market.[28]

AN ALTERNATIVE BANK INSURANCE ARRANGEMENT

An alternative arrangement to the present FDIC insurance scheme is now proposed.   It is recognized that FDIC insurance is a second-best solution in that it is an improvement over an informationally imperfect competitive bank insurance market but falls short of dealing effectively with information problems in a bank insurance market.   In addition, FDIC insurance adversely affects bank liability and asset management. However it is also recognized that bank insurance is necessary to promote a financially sound bank industry.   This discussion, then, focuses on the possibility of classifying bank risk to improve upon the shortcomings of the FDIC arrangement, while providing a stable bank insurance environment.

FDIC insurance indirectly induces banks to take riskier asset (portfolio) positions than they would without it.   And as this chapter's findings reveal, banks can have incentive to face more risk because FDIC premiums are not sensitive to bank risk; all banks belong to the same risk class.   Of course the ability of a bank insurance market to offer risk classes depends on its ability to assess banks' probabilities of failure. If that is too difficult a second-best solution may be warranted (e.g., the current FDIC premium assessments).   If the probability of failure can be properly defined, however, risk class offerings can improve efficiency under the current FDIC regime.

Assessing the probability of failure is far from a simple task.   Bank failures occur for a myriad of reasons, such as inefficient management, riskiness of a bank's portfolio, or depressed economic conditions.   It is useful to divide failures into two categories: controlled and uncontrolled.[29]   Controlled failures are failures that would take place as a result of banks' actions in normal economic times.   Uncontrolled failures are failures that occur independent of bank actions and are due to such events as bank runs during a depression, events that would not occur in normal economic times. Of course it is difficult to define what are normal economic times. However, if banks' risks in terms of controlled failures can be grouped, a viable alternative to the present FDIC insurance scheme becomes possible.

The FDIC should continue to insure all member banks so that uncontrolled as well as controlled failures are insured. However, a different payment system for this insurance coverage is proposed. Consider a two-part tariff scheme where banks first pay an initial payment for participating in the insurance process and then pay a premium for insurance based on their riskiness. Under this arrangement, the initial payment goes into a back-up insurance fund used to pay off claims during uncontrolled bank failures. The initial payment could be assessed on a fraction of total deposits, kD, similar to the way FDIC premiums are assessed today. However, this insurance fund is used only in extreme circumstances (e.g., depressed economic times which result in bank runs). At the end of each year (or a given time period) the FDIC would return the unused funds back to the banks. The money raised by the insurance premiums based on bank risk goes into a primary fund. The primary fund is broken down into smaller funds with each fund specific to a risk group. Each risk group fund then pays off claims for that particular risk group. If bank risk classifications are inaccurate (which is likely during the early stages of risk classification)[30] some risk class funds may be underfunded while some other funds may be over-funded relative to claims. Thus, the FDIC should be allowed to transfer funds from one risk class fund to another in times of need. Under this arrangement, the FDIC may gradually learn how to classify bank risk and eventually each risk class fund could become self-sufficient.

To classify bank risk, the FDIC can use bank risk characteristics, such as portfolio mix, bank size, and capital, that can be monitored by the Federal Reserve or the FDIC. Banks then are given a table indicating the range of all bank characteristics for each given risk class. If a bank's risk characteristics increase such that it now is grouped into a higher risk class, its insurance premiums will increase accordingly.[31] This possibility of bank risk classification is investigated in Chapter 6.

In order to assure efficient risk classifications it may be necessary to introduce a competitive environment for risk classification. One recommendation would be to let another insurance corporation such as the Federal Savings and Loan Insurance Corporation (FSLIC) to compete openly with the FDIC for commercial banks, mutual savings, and saving and loans for insurance coverage. In this way, direct competition between the two federal insurance corporations may lead to more efficient use of resources during the classification process.

The proposed insurance arrangement improves the present FDIC set up in a number of ways. First, under the proposed two-part premium, premiums now are sensitive to bank risk characeristics which are being monitored by the authorities. Thus, banks' risks now are kept in check. Second, the FDIC now classifies banks into their appropriate risk classes which may reduce the market's information problems. In terms of the bank insurance model, i.e., Figure 5.4, this proposed FDIC arrangement is a movement from a pooled c_1 contract offering towards low-risk banks purchasing actuarially fair contracts α^L while high-risk banks purchase actuarially fair contracts α^H. Of course if risk classification is imperfect (a probable occurrence) the FDIC may consider offering separating contracts (e.g., $\alpha^H, \alpha^{L'}$) to induce banks to select themselves into their appropriate risk groups. And finally, this alternative FDIC system continues to assure a financially sound banking environment.

NOTES

1. The loss, L, is the total deposit loss, in dollars, due to bank failure.

2. The zero-profit contract lines EL and EH are identical to the accident insurance zero-profit contract lines, and are thus derived from equations (5) and (8) in Chapter 3.

3. Note that U^L is the indifference curve for depositors in low-risk banks and U^H is the indifference curve for depositors in high-risk banks.

4. In contrast, in the accident insurance market, e.g., automobile insurance, drivers are assumed to know their own probabilities of incurring accident since they can control the way they drive. However, accidents do occur when it is not the fault of the driver and in these cases it is difficult for the driver to assess the probability of accident.

5. For example, an insurance firm may assess a bank's risk based on he riskiness of a bank's portfolio. However, if economic conditions deteriorate, the riskiness of the portfolio may increase.

6. Kleindorfer and Kunreuther (59) introduced consumer misperceptions in the accident insurance market by examining individual's perceived utilities, and we will accordingly do the same for the bank insurance case.

7. See Chapter 3, for a complete development of expected utility.

8. Notice that incomplete information has already been incorporated on the seller side since firms are forced to offer separating contracts.

9. This, of course, is consistent with $P^H_* < P^H$ resulting in flatter high-risk subjective indifference curves.

10. See Chapter 3, footnote 17.

11. The eight possible cases of bank misperceptions about their own bank failures are as follows:

$$P^L_* = P^L, \ P^H_* > P^H; \ P^L_* = P^L, \ P^H_* < P^H; \ P^L_* < P^L, \ P^H_* = P^H; \ P^L_* > L^P, \ P^H_* = P^H;$$

$$P^L_* < P^L, \ P^H_* < P^H; \ P^L_* < P^L, \ P^H_* > P^H; \ P^L_* > P^L, \ P^H_* < P^H; \ P^L_* > P^L, \ P^H_* > P^H.$$

12. This scenario is similar to Akerlof's market for lemons (1).

13. This assumption will be relaxed later in the analysis.

14. Recognize that banks may vary in size not only between low-risk and high-risk banks, but also within the low-risk and high-risk banks, but also within the low-risk and high-risk groups. However, banks of varying sizes still pay the same insurance rate per unit of coverage since each bank pays the same $k per unit of deposit and every bank purchases $100,000 deposit coverage.

15.   For a more thorough account of FDIC operations, see Chapter 1.

16.   This is similar to the finding in our previous analysis where depositors purchase contract c_1 in Figure 5.4

17.   The FDIC does offer a premium that is close to being actuarially fair to the entire bank insurance market. This was discussed earlier in this section.

18.   These assumptions are made for simplicity. Assumed away are time deposits, required reserves, cash flow costs, government bonds, etc.. These could easily be included without altering our results.

19.   Thus, in this model D–L = required reserves.

20.   It is recognized that through the Depository Monetary Control of 1980 passed by Congress, Regulation Q now is slowly being phased out of binding power.

21.   The derivation of the efficient frontier can be found in most finance text books, such as Fama (29) and Lorrie and Hamilton (65).

22.   Since we assume for now that funds are not procured by issuing deposits, it is assumed that banks' initial investment capital, equity, is available for portfolio investment.

23.   Since $R_D > R_f$, banks shy away from lending. Purchases of riskless assets probably occur for liquidity or regulatory reasons.

24.   This will be true for most individual customers. Large corporations are probably the only exceptions.

25.   Actually depositors now pay an insurance premium in the form of receiving a lower interest rate on their deposits. Thus, this premium might contribute to a movement from R_D to an interest rate below R_f. This possibility is discussed later in the analysis.

26.   For a detailed presentation of this analysis, see Epps (37).

27.   Recall, in Figure 5.6 an excess demand for funds is associated with Regulation Q.   Thus, there might exist a decrease in the amount of funds acquired by deposits as a result of Regulation Q.   However, This analysis does not depend on an absolute amount but only on relative proportions.

28.   However, it may be that when the presence of FDIC insurance eliminates risk for depositors, the interest rate, R_D they receive on their deposits (which reflects the insurance premium) is equal to the riskless rate R_f on assets.   This is because if the financial markets are competitive, two investments with the same degree of risk (in this case riskless) must in equilibrium pay the same interest payment, $R_D = R_f$.

29.   Gibson (37) suggest there are normal and depression failures.   The headings controlled and uncontrolled are chosen so as not to suggest that depressions are the sole characteristic of uncontrolled failures.   For example, hyper–inflation or wars may lead to eventual bank failure independently of bank action.

30. It may take time for the FDIC to accurately classify bank risk. They will have to expand resources, time and energy to collect data in order to study, formulate, and test risk classifications.

31. The FDIC has proposed a modest risk-related premium system that would have only three risk categories: normal, high and very high risk. Under the program, most banks would be categorized into the normal risk class. Risk classification would be based only on credit risk, interest rate risk and capital adequacy. This proposal is outlined in the FDIC deposit insurance study (31).

6

Bank Risk Classification

INTRODUCTION

This chapter presents an empirical investigation into the
possibility of commercial bank risk classification. In order to
estimate a vector of bank risk characteristics, logit analysis
is performed on a sample of commercial banks consisting of
failed commercial banks and a random sample of solvent commercial banks. These banks are then grouped into risk classes
based on their characteristics and the classification process
is tested on a holdout sample. The empirical findings indicate
that financial ratios are the most important variables in predicting bank failure. However, other variables, such as the
number of bank branches, city vs. country bank, and regulatory
status (membership in the Federal Reserve system) also aid in
explaining differences between failed and solvent banks.

The chapter begins with a brief review of previous studies
on the prediction of bank failure and the development of bank
early warning systems. This study's methodology is then
explained with a description of the logit procedure used. The
chapter proceeds with an account of the data and the explanatory variables used and a presentation of the empirical findings. Finally, some conclusions and a discussion for future
research are offered.

PREVIOUS STUDIES

The first serious attempt at predicting bank failure was
carried out by Meyer and Pifer (76). Their study set out to

discriminate between failed and solvent banks that face similar
local and national market conditions. Their sample included 39
pairs of failed banks and comparable solvent banks during the
period 1948 to 1965. Least squares regressions were performed
on models which contained a dichotomous dependent variable.
Their findings revealed that certain financial variables
reflect managerial ability and employee honesty and therefore
can be used one or two years prior to failure to distinguish
solvent banks from failed banks due to poor management and/or
embezzlement.

Other recent attempts at predicting bank failure include
Sinkey (98), (99); Sinkey and Walker (100); Rose and Scott
(91); and Pettway and Sinkey (83) and Bovenzi, Marino and
McFadden (17). In each study statistical analyses were conducted to distinguish financial characteristics between a group
of failed or identified problem banks and a comparable group of
solvent banks. For example, Sinkey (98) performed a multivariate statistical analysis on a sample of banks which
consisted of 110 problem banks identified in 1972 and 1973 and
a matched sample of 110 non-problem banks. The analysis identified financial ratios which distinguished problem banks from
non-problem banks.

Sinkey and Walker (100) also performed statistical tests
on a problem bank group and a comparable nonproblem bank group.
Specifically, they developed an early-warning system to screen
problem banks (defined by the FDIC). Analysis of variance
tests were applied to financial data for the 62 banks on the
FDIC problem list in 1972 and to a comparable 62 bank group.
Their study concluded that the average problem bank could be
identified (by observing certain financial ratios) at least a
year before the bank examination process identified them.

In another study Rose and Scott(91) analyzed the financial
data for two bank groups consisting of 69 commercial banks that
failed during the years 1965-1975 and a comparable-sized solvent bank group during the same time period. Multivariate
statistical tests revealed significant differences in financial
ratios between failed and comparable solvent banks. And, more
recently, Pettway and Sinkey (83) used accounting data and market information to develop an early-warning system to screen
problem banks from a group of large banks with actively traded
securities. Their examination of only large banks was justified on the grounds that failures of large banks present
the greatest risk to the bank insurance fund and consequently
to the stability of the banking system. Their study found that
by using an early-warning system which includes both accounting
and market information, six of the largest banks which subsequently failed would have been classified as problem banks
at least one year before the beginning of the classifying
examination.

Recently, Bovenzi, Marino, and McFadden (17) developed
bank failure prediction models to analyze failure probabilities

for about 1400 insured commercial banks, covering failures that
occurred between 1980 and 1983. The additional predictive value
of exam report data was tested.   The ability of models to predict failure up to 3 years in advance was tested. In addition,
model estimation efficiency was compared with sample estimates
both with and without weighting to compensate for the difference in sampling rates between failures and non-failures.

To summarize, previous studies have   established the
usefulness of statistical analysis on acounting data in identifying problem and/or failed banks. It appears then that some
financial ratios may reflect embezzlement and fraud, reasons
usually given for bank failure.   Most studies also employ
similar methodologies; financial ratios from a sample of problem   or failed banks are statistically compared with
financial ratios from a comparable sample of solvent banks, the
sample banks are then reclassified and a holdout sample is used
to test the study's predictive capabilities.

METHODOLOGY

Our objective is not simply to predict bank failures or
identify problem banks, but to classify banks into risk groups
according to their probabilities of failure.   An attempt is
made to identify the bank characteristics that help place banks
into distinguishable risk groups.   That is bank risk classification is treated similar to accident risk classification. For
example, in automobile insurance, insurance firms use individual characteristics, such as age, sex, neighborhood, and past
driving record, in an attempt to classify customers into risk
groups.   For bank insurance, bank characteristics, such as the
number of bank branches, regulatory status, bank size, and local market environment, as well as the use of financial ratios
are used in an attempt to classify banks into risk groups.

This attempt at bank risk classification proceeds in the
following manner. Logit analysis is performed on a sample of
commercial banks consisting of failed commercial banks and a
random sample[1] of solvent commercial banks in order to estimate
the regression

(1)   Y = XB + e

where Y is a dichotomous dependent variable (0,1) which takes
on a value of 1 for a failed bank and 0 for a solvent bank, X
is vector of bank characteristics which includes bank financial
ratios in addition to other risk characteristics, and e is a
random disturbance. This investigation differs from most previous studies because a group of failed banks is contrasted
with a random sample of solvent banks instead of contrasting a
failed bank group with a comparable solvent bank group.   And
included are other distinguishing bank characteristics, e.g.,

regulatory environment, in addition to financial data which was the only concern of previous studies. The application of logit analysis also is an improved regression technique over some studies (e.g., Meyer and Pifer (74) estimated by ordinary least squares a regression function which included a dichotomous dependent variable). Contributions of the logit procedure are discussed in the following sections.

Maximum likelihood estimates of the vector of bank characteristics, X, are used to create an index of riskiness for banks. Coefficient estimates will generate the probability of bank failure for each bank within the next year. The distribution of these fitted values can be used to determine risk classes. This classification process is then tested on a holdout sample.

THE LOGIT PROCEDURE

Consider the regression model

$$(1) \qquad\qquad Y = XB + e$$

where there are only two possible states of the world, failure and no failure (solvency). The dependent variable Y takes on the values 1 or 0 corresponding to the two states. If the fact that Y is dichotomous is ignored and if we estimate (1), it follows that e, given X, can take on only two values $(1 - XB)$ and $-XB$. Hence, employing a least squares procedure violates the assumptions that the residuals are normally distributed and have a constant variance (homoskedasticity). Further, estimation of (1) may result in the right-hand side taking on a value larger than 1 or smaller than 0, while Y cannot lie outside the (0,1) interval. It is obvious that a better estimation procedure is needed to rectify the complications that arise from direct estimation of (1).

The logit procedure is a common estimation technique performed on models containing a dichotomous endogenous variable such as (1) so that the observed values of Y are treated as a realization of a probability process. That is in order for the disturbance term, e, to have zero expectation for a given X, it should take the value $-BX$ with probability $1 - BX$ and the value $1 - BX$ with probability BX. However, since a probability is confined to the interval (0,1) it is inconsistent with most regressions. Thus a monotonic transformation is applied to the probability so that (0,1) is transformed to $(-\infty, \infty)$. The logit and the probit transformations are the most widely used. The probit transformation assumes that e has a cumulative normal, $F(BX)$, while the logit transformation assumes $F(BX)$ is the logistic $e^{BX}/1+e^{BX}$. The logit procedure is the monotonic transformation, $\log p/1-p$, where p is a probability.

Regarding estimation, the procedure employed in this study is a stepwise logistic procedure that selects independent variables in a stepwise manner, and estimates the coefficients for a logistic regression.[2]   The dependent variable is a binary variable that takes on a value of 0 or 1. The predicted proportion of successes (s/n) follows the logistic model $\exp(U)/1 + \exp(U)$ where s is the sum of the binary (0,1) dependent variable, n is the total sample size, and U is a linear function of one or more independent variables. At each step in the stepwise process, a variable is added to or removed from the model.   The set of coefficients, B, for the included terms are estimated as the value that maximizes the likelihood function. After estimating B, a decision is made whether to enter or remove any term in the next step.   This decision is based on an estimate of the asymptotic covariance matrix of B. F-values are obtained and the tail area of probabilities are computed.   Terms are then removed or entered depending on prespecified p-value limits.   The maximum likelihood estimates are computed by an iterative process (Jennrich and Moore (51)).

THE DATA AND EXPLANATORY VARIABLES

The main source of data used in this study came from commercial bank data tapes supply by the Federal Deposit Insurance Corporation (FDIC).   Each FDIC data tape includes a Consolidated Report of Income and a Consolidated Report of Condition for each commercial bank operating in the United States.   Tapes supplied were for the years 1978, 1979, and 1980. A random sample of 277 banks from a population of 14,404 banks was selected from the 1978 data tape with the criterion that these banks be solvent in 1979.[3]   Also selected were 7 other banks from the 1978 tape that eventually failed in 1979.[4] Thus this test sample of 284 banks included financial information in 1978 in which 7 of these banks failed in the following year.

In this attempt at bank risk classification, bank characteristics, such as the number of bank branches, regulatory status, city vs. country, and bank size, as well as financial ratios are used.   The financial ratios to be tested include those that have been meaningful in previous studies ((76), (98) and (85)).   Each ratio is designed to reflect some part of a bank's operation and performance.   The following is a list of the explanatory variables employed:[5]

X_1 = total operating expenses/total operating income, a measure of a bank's operating efficiency,

X_2 = loans/capital, a measure of capital adequacy,

X_3 = cash + United States and other securities/assets, a measure of liquidity safety for risk,

X_4 = loans/assets, reflects risk exposure,

X_5 = income from loans/total operating income, measures a source of revenue,

X_6 = interest paid on deposits/total operating income, measures a use of revenue,

X_7 = other expenses/total operating income, measures a use of revenue

X_8 = assets/average assets for sample, and index for bank size.

X_9 = time and savings deposits/demand deposits,

X_{10} = total number of branches for each bank,

X_{11} = (0,1) dummy variable where X_{11} takes on a value of 1 if observation is a nonmember bank of the Federal Reserve System and 0 if it is a member bank,

X_{12} = (0,1) dummy variable where X_{12} takes on a value of 1 if observation is a country bank and 0 if it is a city bank (a country bank is defined to be a bank operating within a county with a population less than 100,000 people).[6]

The stepwise logistic procedure is then applied to the model

(2) $Y = B_0 + B_1 X_1 + B_2 X_2 + \ldots + B_{12} X_{12} + e$,

where Y is a (0,1) binary variable and X_1 through X_{12} are the explanatory variables listed above. The empirical results are presented in the next section.

EMPIRICAL FINDINGS

The logit-analysis tests presented in this section show that financial ratios are still the most important variables in predicting bank failure. That is, even when other bank characteristics are included such as regulatory status, number branches, and city vs. country status, financial ratios continue to dominate the regressions. The regression results for equation (2) are presented in Tables 6.1 and 6.2. Recall that a stepwise logistic procedure is employed so only the variables selected by the procedure are included in the final regression.

Table 6.1 presents the regression results from the original sample of 284 banks of which 7 eventually failed the following year. Similarly, Table 6.2 presents the regression results from an enlarged sample group of 291 banks. Of these banks, 284 are from the original sample and the remaining 7 banks were taken from the 1979 data tape. The criterion for selecting these 7 banks was that each bank must eventually fail the following year (1980). Thus, this expanded sample contains 1978 data for 7 banks that eventually fail in 1979 and 1979 data for 7 banks that eventually fail in 1980. By including the latter group in the sample, these banks are treated as if they had reported 1978 data and failed in 1979. Thus it is implicitly assumed that there is no significant change in the X_1 through X_{12} variables due to a one year change in time. This assumption allows us to increase the number of failed observations (from 7 to 14) in the sample. In each table the number of independent variables depends on the stepwise logistic procedure so they may differ from each other.

In Tables 6.1 and 6.2, for each variable the regression coefficient, its standard error and the coefficient divided by its standard error (a t-value) are presented. And for each regression two tests that measure the goodness–of–fit of the model are included. The Hosmer Goodness-of-Fit test compares the observed and predicted frequency of 10 cells. Cells are defined by the predicted values. A small p-value means that the predicted values do not fit the data. The C. C. Brown Goodness-of-Fit test compares the fit of data to the logistic model. A small p-value indicates that the logistic model is not appropriate for the data.

For the 284 bank sample (Table 6.1), variables X_1, X_3, X_4, X_5, X_6, X_7, X_{11}, and X_{12} were included as a result of the stepwise procedure. The sign and significance of these variables are now explained.

Variable X_1 = total operating expenses/total operating income. The coefficient is positive and significant at least at the 1 percent level. The positive sign indicates that the value of X_1 is significantly greater for failed banks than for solvent banks. In other words, banks that eventually fail are less efficient than solvent banks.

Variable X_3 = cash + U.S. and other securities/assets. Surprisingly this measure of liquidity is not significant in distinguishing failed from solvent banks.

Variable X_4 = loans/assets. The coefficient is positive and significant at least at the 2.5 per cent level. The positive sign indicates that the value of X_4 is significantly greater for failed banks than for solvent banks. Thus this variable indicates banks that eventually fail are exposed to more risk than banks that remain solvent.

Variable X_5 = income from loans/total operating income. The coefficient is negative and is significant at least at the

TABLE 6.1

Parameter Estimates For 284 Bank Sample

Variable	Coefficient	Standard Error	Coeff./S.E.
X_1	15.086	6.215	2.427
X_3	-9.699	16.503	-0.588
X_4	50.713	23.559	2.153
X_5	-41.516	21.398	-1.940
X_6	4.703	9.082	0.510
X_7	18.333	10.860	1.688
X_{11}	-2.168	1.339	-1.619
X_{12}	-1.697	1.232	-1.377
Constant	-25.170	13.697	-1.838

p-value (D. Hosmer) = 0.646
p-value (C.C. Brown) = 0.358

149

TABLE 6.2

Parameter Estimates for 291 Bank Sample

Variable	Coefficient	Standard Error	Coeff./S.E.
X_1	3.045	1.511	2.015
X_2	0.680	0.215	3.170
X_3	10.418	8.879	1.173
X_4	33.281	12.671	2.627
X_5	-7.770	9.319	-0.834
X_6	-6.304	4.822	-1.320
X_7	18.689	8.524	2.193
X_9	0.939	0.428	2.192
X_{10}	-0.529	0.371	-1.425
X_{12}	-0.859	-0.636	-1.351
Constant	-33.280	10.981	-3.031

p-value (D. Hosmer) = 0.301
p-value (C.C. Brown) = 0.577

5 percent level. The negative sign indicates that the value of X_5 is significantly less for failed banks than for solvent banks. That is, for failed banks income from loans represents a lower proportion of total income earned than for solvent banks. This may reflect the poor loan strategies for failed banks.

Variable X_6 = interest paid on deposits/total operating income. The variable represents a use of revenue that is not found to be significant in the regression.

Variable X_7 = other expenses/total operating income. The coefficient is positive and significant at least at the 5 percent level. The positive sign indicates that failed banks spend a higher proportion of their revenue on 'other' expenses (other than interest paid on deposits).

Variable X_{11} = (0,1) dummy variable which represents member and non-member banks of the Federal Reserve system. The coefficient is negative and significant at least of the 10 percent level. The negative sign indicates that a nonmember bank is less likely to fail, a curious finding since we do not observe a higher percentage of failed banks being member banks.

Variable X_{12} = (0,1) dummy variable which represents city vs. country banks. The coefficient is negative and significant at least at the 10 percent level. The negative sign indicated that country banks are less likely to fail than city banks.

For the 291 bank sample (Table 6.2), variables X_1, X_2, X_3, X_4, X_5, X_6, X_7, X_9, X_{10}, and X_{12} were included as a result of the stepwise procedure. Thus variables X_2, X_9, and X_{10} passed the stepwise process for this sample while failing to make the cut in the original sample (Table 6.1). And X_{11} included in the original sample is not included in this sample's regression. The sign and significance of the variables included in both regressions can be briefly discussed, and attention will be focused on differences from the other regression.

Variable X_1 -- still has a positive coefficient and is significant at least at the 5 percent level or better.

Variable X_2 = loans/capital.   The coefficient here is positive and significant at least at the 2.5 percent level, although it was not included in Table 6.1. The positive sign indicates that failed banks have significantly lower levels of capital adequacy than do solvent banks.

Variable X_3, a measure of liquidity and insignificant in the previous regression, is still insignificant.

Variable X_4 -- still has a positive coefficient and is significant at least at the .5 per cent level.

Variable X_5 -- is now insignificant.

Variable X_6 -- insignificant in the previous regression, now has a negative coefficient and is significant at the 10 percent level. The negative sign indicates that the value of X_6 is less for failed banks than for solvent banks.

Variable X_7 -- still has a positive coefficient and is significant at the 5 percent level.

Variable X_9 = time and saving deposits/demand deposits, was not included in Table 6.1. The coefficient is positive and significant at the 2.5 percent level. The positive sign indicates that the value of X_9 is greater for failed banks than for solvent banks. The positive relationship between this ratio and the likelihood of failure might be attributed to the difference in costs of demand and time deposits.

Variable X_{10} = total number of branches, was not included in Table 6.1. The coefficient is negative and significant at least at the 10 per cent level. The negative sign indicates that banks with a high branch number are less likely to fail.

Variable X_{13} -- still has a negative sign and is at least significant at the 10 per cent level.

The regression results from the test samples are consistent with findings of previous studies and with our prior knowledge about what distinguishes failed banks from solvent banks. Financial ratios are still the best discriminators; failed banks face more risk exposure, are less efficient (profitable) and possess less adequate capital than solvent banks. It is also interesting to note that a country bank is less likely to fail than a city bank and a bank with many branches is less likely to fail than a bank with few or no branches. Also note that variable, X_8 was excluded from the reported regressions as a result of the stepwise procedure.

Although they differ in the inclusion of some explanatory variables both regression models have similar predictions for the probabilty of bank failure (i.e., the estimated $\hat{Y}$) for each observation (bank) in their test sample. The findings of the 291 bank test sample in are reported in Table 6.3 below. The table lists for each observation whether it is a failed or solvent bank and its predicted probability of failure. A cursory look at the bank table reveals that most solvent banks are associated with extremely low predicted probabilities of failure, while most failed banks (the last 14 observations) are associated with high predicted probabilities of failure.

In order to convey the dispersion of predicted probabilities, the histograms of predicted probabilities of failure for both solvent and failed bank groups are plotted in Figures 6.1 and 6.2. Figure 6.1 reveals that out of the 14 failed banks in our sample, 10 have predicted probabilities of failure of greater than 50 percent, 1 bank has over a 30 percent predicted probability of failure (still a high probability compared with solvent banks' probabilities), 1 bank has over a 17 percent predicted probability of failure and 2 banks have very low predicted probabilities of failure. On the other hand, Figure 6.2 reveals that most solvent banks have extremely low predicted probabilities of failure (clustering around the zero probability range). A relatively small number of solvent banks have higher predicted probabilities of failure but there are few banks near the .67 predicted probability range.

Let us now group these sample banks into risk classes based on their predicted probabilities of failure. Table 6.4 presents the correct classifications resulting from placing different cut-off points on the computed predicted probabilities of failure (presented in Table 6.3). Column 1 presents the cut-off points ranging from .008 to .992. Columns 2, 3, and 4 present the number of correct predictions for failed banks, solvent banks and their totals. Columns 5, 6, and 7 present the percentage of correct predictions for the failed group, the solvent group, and their total percentage (of all banks). The table was constructed from Table 6.3 in the following manner. An observation is predicted to be in the solvent group if its probability is less than or equal to the cut-off point. Similarly, an observation is predicted to be in the failed group if its probability is greater than the cut-off point. For example, if the cut-off point were .008, column 1 indicates that all 14 failed banks' predicted probabilities of failure lie above this cut-off point and are thus correctly classified into the failed group. Similarly, column 2 indicates that 231 solvent banks have predicted probabilities of failure equal to or less than the cut-off point and are classified into the solvent group. Thus, as column 3 reveals, 245 banks were correctly classified for an 84.19 percent rating (column 7).

Risk classes are constructed by selecting those cut-off point ranges that minimize a type 1 error. A type 1 error occurs when a bank which subsequently fails is predicted to be a solvent bank (in our case if the failed bank is predicted to have a low probability). A type 11 error occurs whenever a solvent bank is assumed to be failing. Table 6.5 presents the risk classifications constructed based on this procedure. As a result of this procedure 6 risk classes emerge, A through F. The table lists for each risk class, A-F, its cut-off point range and the composition of its members. For example, the classification process places 231 solvent banks and zero failed banks in the lowest risk class group, A, defined by the cut-off point range, .000 -.008, and the highest risk class group, F, defined by the cut-off range, .4921-1.00, contains 3 solvent banks and 10 failed banks.[7]

This classification process is now tested on a holdout sample. This sample is a 12 bank sample taken from the 1980 FDIC data tape and is composed of 6 failed banks (banks that subsequently failed in 1981) and 6 solvent banks randomly chosen.[8] Thus it is assumed economic conditions are stable over the time period of this study. Table 6.6 presents the predicted probabilities the model assigns to each holdout bank. For each observation, the Table lists the type of bank (failed or solvent), bank name, predicted probability, and assigned risk class. The findings reveal good predictive ability. Of the 6 failed banks in the sample, 5 were assigned to the highest risk class, F, (an 83 percent accuracy) while the remaining failed bank was assigned to a lower but still high risk class, D. And of the 6 solvent banks, 5 were assigned to the lowest risk class, A, while the remaining solvent bank was assigned to the second lowest risk class, B.

CONCLUSION

This chapter represents a preliminary investigation into the possibility of commercial bank risk classification. In an attempt at classification bank characteristics, such as the number of bank branches, regulatory status, city vs. country banks, and bank size as well as the use of financial ratios are used. Although financial ratios appear to dominate the regression, bank branches and city vs. country variables offered explanatory contributions to the model. However, there are limitations to the model and an obvious need for improvement. For example, the city vs. country variable is used as a proxy for a bank's local market condition. Income per capita for a bank's county or an index of economic condition by county are probably better proxies for local market condition.[9] Further, the variable bank size was expected to be significant in discriminating failed from solvent banks since most failed banks observed are small. An expanded sample size might improve the explanatory power of bank size.

Finally, the implementation of a commercial bank risk classification system prompts several comments. Most importantly, although the goal of a risk-premium FDIC insurance scheme is to inhibit bank riskiness, it may have the perverse effect of increasing a bank's probability of failure. For example, under such a scheme, once banks are classified into their appropriate risk classes, they are given a table indicating the range of all bank characteristics for each given risk class. If a potential failing bank's risk characteristics increase such that it is now grouped into a higher risk class, its insurance premium will increase accordingly. The increased insurance cost now worsens the bank's operating position making it more vulnerable to failure. However, once the risk-premium insurance scheme is operational, it should inhibit banks from risk taking so that banks would have incentive not to place themselves in the position of vulnerability.

Second, if the FDIC were to adopt a system of risk-related deposit insurance premiums, the above findings should serve only as a guide for risk classification. The 291 bank test sample is small in contrast to the approximately 15,000 commercial banks operating in the United States today. Any serious attempt at bank classification should include a larger sample (preferably all 15,000 banks) and a longer time period.

Third, if a viable risk classification system is to be taken seriously, the costs of misclassification must be considered. Inefficient classification may result in a misallocation of resources. That is if low-risk banks are classified as high-risk banks, they are forced to pay premiums that are greater than what is actuarially fair. And if high-risk banks (banks that eventually fail) are classified as low-risk banks, substantial risks to the bank insurance fund now exist and consequently to the stability of the banking system. Bank classification may be approachable but its applicability may still not be practical. It is obvious that more research is needed in this area.

TABLE 6.3

Predicted Probabilities of Failure

Obs.	Failed	Solvent	Pred. Prob.of Failure	Obs.	Failed	Solvent	Pred. Prob.of Failure
1	0	1	.0000	40	0	1	.0011
2	0	1	.0000	41	0	1	.0008
3	0	1	.0000	42	0	1	.0207
4	0	1	.0000	43	0	1	.0014
5	0	1	.0000	44	0	1	.0074
6	0	1	.0000	45	0	1	.0000
7	0	1	.0000	46	0	1	.0000
8	0	1	.0000	47	0	1	.0475
9	0	1	.0000	48	0	1	.0062
10	0	1	.0000	49	0	1	.0000
11	0	1	.0000	50	0	1	.0000
12	0	1	.0000	51	0	1	.0000
13	0	1	.0000	52	0	1	.0000
14	0	1	.0000	53	0	1	.0067
15	0	1	.0011	54	0	1	.0044
16	0	1	.0000	55	0	1	.0000
17	0	1	.0001	56	0	1	.0014
18	0	1	.0000	57	0	1	.0002
19	0	1	.0000	58	0	1	.0003
20	0	1	.0000	59	0	1	.0000
21	0	1	.0019	60	0	1	.0001
22	0	1	.0052	61	0	1	.0000
23	0	1	.0000	62	0	1	.0000
24	0	1	.0000	63	0	1	.0004
25	0	1	.0000	64	0	1	.0094
26	0	1	.0000	65	0	1	.0004
27	0	1	.0041	66	0	1	.0261
28	0	1	.0002	67	0	1	.0000
29	0	1	.0002	68	0	1	.0008
30	0	1	.0000	69	0	1	.0004
31	0	1	.0000	70	0	1	.0038
32	0	1	.0151	71	0	1	.0001
33	0	1	.0000	72	0	1	.0000
34	0	1	.0000	73	0	1	.0027
35	0	1	.0000	74	0	1	.0000
36	0	1	.0001	75	0	1	.0001
37	0	1	.0015	76	0	1	.0000
38	0	1	.0000	77	0	1	.0001
39	0	1	.0000	78	0	1	.0014

Table 6.3 cont'd

Obs.	Failed	Solvent	Pred. Prob.of Failure	Obs.	Failed	Solvent	Pred. Prob.of Failure
79	0	1	.0040	124	0	1	.0000
80	0	1	.0006	125	0	1	.0000
81	0	1	.0821	126	0	1	.0000
82	0	1	.0002	127	0	1	.0006
83	0	1	.0000	128	0	1	.0002
84	0	1	.0004	129	0	1	.0010
85	0	1	.0000	130	0	1	.0006
86	0	1	.0007	131	0	1	.0126
87	0	1	.0030	132	0	1	.0074
88	0	1	.0000	133	0	1	.0001
89	0	1	.0002	134	0	1	.0015
90	0	1	.0018	135	0	1	.0780
91	0	1	.0002	136	0	1	.0001
92	0	1	.0000	137	0	1	.0015
93	0	1	.0001	138	0	1	.0000
94	0	1	.0061	139	0	1	.0002
95	0	1	.0000	140	0	1	.0016
96	0	1	.0001	141	0	1	.0775
97	0	1	.0089	142	0	1	.0005
98	0	1	.0000	143	0	1	.0003
99	0	1	.0001	144	0	1	.0002
100	0	1	.0137	145	0	1	.0000
101	0	1	.0000	146	0	1	.0000
102	0	1	.0005	147	0	1	.0006
103	0	1	.0002	148	0	1	.0000
104	0	1	.0000	149	0	1	.0015
105	0	1	.0000	150	0	1	.0148
106	0	1	.0000	151	0	1	.0012
107	0	1	.0012	152	0	1	.0009
108	0	1	.0000	153	0	1	.0000
109	0	1	.0000	154	0	1	.0000
110	0	1	.0000	155	0	1	.0024
111	0	1	.0019	156	0	1	.0105
112	0	1	.0014	157	0	1	.0001
113	0	1	.0000	158	0	1	.0050
114	0	1	.0000	159	0	1	.0041
115	0	1	.0314	160	0	1	.0000
116	0	1	.0001	161	0	1	.0134
117	0	1	.0000	162	0	1	.0295
118	0	1	.0000	163	0	1	.0000
119	0	1	.0000	164	0	1	.0001
120	0	1	.0001	165	0	1	.0001
121	0	1	.0001	166	0	1	.0008
122	0	1	.0000	167	0	1	.0020
123	0	1	.0000	168	0	1	.0053

Table 6.3 cont'd

Obs.	Failed	Solvent	Pred. Prob.of Failure	Obs.	Failed	Solvent	Pred. Prob.of Failure
169	0	1	.0042	213	0	1	.0003
170	0	1	.0000	214	0	1	.0000
171	0	1	.0000	215	0	1	.0000
172	0	1	.0002	216	0	1	.0000
173	0	1	.0003	217	0	1	.0027
174	0	1	.0002	218	0	1	.0017
175	0	1	.0002	219	0	1	.0108
176	0	1	.0026	220	0	1	.2734
177	0	1	.0080	221	0	1	.0002
178	0	1	.0000	222	0	1	.0000
179	0	1	.0018	223	0	1	.0019
180	0	1	.0827	224	0	1	.0022
181	0	1	.0088	225	0	1	.0133
182	0	1	.0002	226	0	1	.0053
183	0	1	.0000	227	0	1	.0006
184	0	1	.0001	228	0	1	.0030
185	0	1	.0001	229	0	1	.0000
186	0	1	.0005	230	0	1	.0000
187	0	1	.0007	231	0	1	.0018
188	0	1	.0005	232	0	1	.0000
189	0	1	.0349	233	0	1	.0066
190	0	1	.0000	234	0	1	.0001
191	0	1	.0017	235	0	1	.0178
192	0	1	.0154	236	0	1	.0000
193	0	1	.0000	237	0	1	.0000
194	0	1	.0058	238	0	1	.0072
195	0	1	.0066	239	0	1	.6681
196	0	1	.0000	240	0	1	.0000
197	0	1	.0002	241	0	1	.4369
198	0	1	.0005	242	0	1	.0001
199	0	1	.0001	243	0	1	.0041
200	0	1	.0006	244	0	1	.0064
201	0	1	.0579	245	0	1	.0081
202	0	1	.0008	246	0	1	.0000
203	0	1	.0003	247	0	1	.1041
204	0	1	.0001	248	0	1	.0010
205	0	1	.0274	249	0	1	.0019
206	0	1	.0001	250	0	1	.0010
207	0	1	.0021	251	0	1	.0022
208	0	1	.0066	252	0	1	.0447
209	0	1	.0005	253	0	1	.0758
210	0	1	.0198	254	0	1	.0000
211	0	1	.0000	255	0	1	.0208
212	0	1	.0040	256	0	1	.0000

Table 6.3 (continued)

Obs.	Failed	Solvent	Pred. Prob.of Failure
257	0	1	.5305
258	0	1	.2183
259	0	1	.0004
260	0	1	.0000
261	0	1	.0000
262	0	1	.0178
263	0	1	.1541
264	0	1	.0012
265	0	1	.1984
266	0	1	.0009
267	0	1	.0000
268	0	1	.0075
269	0	1	.2897
270	0	1	.1478
271	0	1	.0002
272	0	1	.1238
273	0	1	.1139
274	0	1	.3144
275	0	1	.0001
276	0	1	.5752
277	0	1	.4490
278	1	0	.1876
279	1	0	.3781
280	1	0	.9976
281	1	0	.0505
282	1	0	.5064
283	1	0	.0182
284	1	0	.6094
285	1	0	.5480
286	1	0	.7007
287	1	0	.6797
288	1	0	.7028
289	1	0	.9987
290	1	0	.7628
291	1	0	.8861

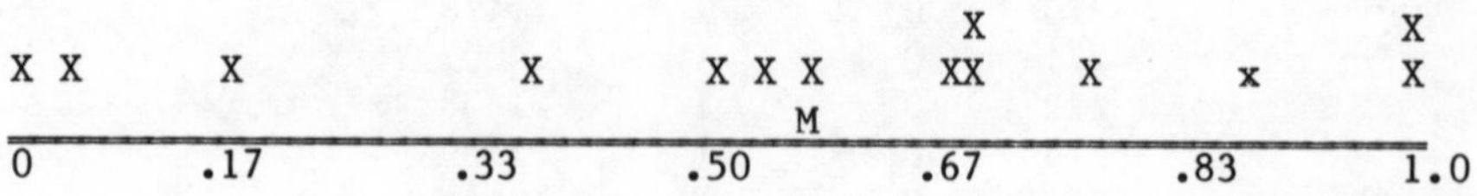

```
                                                X               X
X X      X              X         X X X        XX      X      x      X
                                                                     X
                                           M
0        .17           .33        .50          .67          .83     1.0
```

NOTE: Each X represents 1 Observation
        M Marks the Median

FIGURE 6.1

Histogram of Predicted Probabilities of
Failure for Failed Banks

160

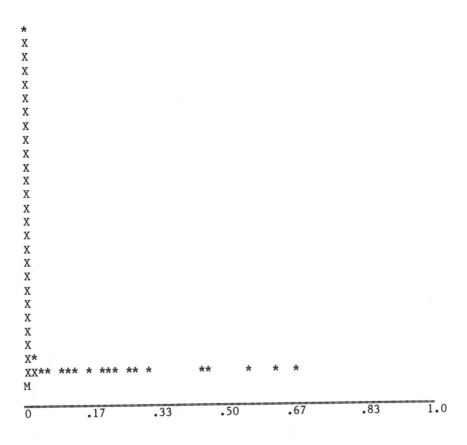

```
*
X
X
X
X
X
X
X
X
X
X
X
X
X
X
X
X
X
X
X
X
X
X
X
X
X*
XX** *** * *** ** *        **      *    *    *
M
0       .17        .33        .50        .67        .83       1.0
```

NOTE: Each X Represents 10 Observations
        Each * Represents Fewer than 10 Observations
        M Marks the Median

FIGURE 6.2

Histogram of Predicted Probabilities of Failure
for Solvent Banks

161

TABLE 6.4

Correct Cut-Off Point Classifications

Cut-Off Point	Correct Pred. Failed	Correct Pred. Solvent	Total	Percent Failed	Correct Solvent	Total
.008	14	231	245	100.00	83.39	84.19
.025	13	248	261	92.86	89.53	89.69
.042	13	253	266	92.86	91.34	91.41
.058	12	256	268	85.71	92.42	92.10
.075	12	256	268	85.71	92.42	92.10
.092	12	260	272	85.71	93.86	93.47
.108	12	262	274	85.71	94.58	94.16
.125	12	264	276	85.71	95.31	94.85
.142	12	264	276	85.71	95.31	94.85
.158	12	266	278	85.71	96.03	95.53
.175	12	266	278	85.71	96.03	95.53
.192	11	267	278	78.57	96.39	95.53
.208	11	268	279	78.57	96.75	95.88
.225	11	269	280	78.57	97.11	96.22
.242	11	269	280	78.57	97.11	96.22
.258	11	269	280	78.57	97.11	96.22
.275	11	270	281	78.57	97.47	96.56
.292	11	271	282	78.57	97.83	96.91
.308	11	271	282	78.57	97.83	96.91
.325	11	272	283	78.57	98.19	97.25
.342	11	272	283	78.57	98.19	97.25
.358	11	272	283	78.57	98.19	97.25
.375	11	272	283	78.57	98.19	97.25
.392	10	272	282	71.43	98.19	96.91
.408	10	272	282	71.43	98.19	96.91
.425	10	272	282	71.43	98.19	96.91
.442	10	273	283	71.43	98.56	97.25
.458	10	274	284	71.43	98.92	97.59
.475	10	274	284	71.43	98.92	97.59
.492	10	274	284	71.43	98.92	97.59
.508	9	274	283	64.29	98.92	97.25
.525	9	274	283	64.29	98.92	97.25
.542	9	275	284	64.29	99.28	97.59
.558	8	275	283	57.14	99.28	97.25
.575	8	275	283	57.14	99.28	97.25

Table 6.4 Cont'd

Cut-Off Point	Correct Pred. Failed	Correct Pred. Solvent	Total	Percent Correct Failed	Percent Correct Solvent	Total
.592	8	276	284	57.14	99.64	97.59
.608	8	276	284	57.14	99.64	97.59
.625	7	276	283	50.00	99.64	97.25
.642	7	276	283	50.00	99.64	97.25
.658	7	276	283	50.00	99.64	97.25
.675	7	277	284	50.00	100.00	97.59
.692	6	277	283	42.86	100.00	97.25
.708	4	277	281	28.57	100.00	96.56
.725	4	277	281	28.57	100.00	96.56
.742	4	277	281	28.57	100.00	96.56
.758	4	277	281	28.57	100.00	96.56
.775	3	277	280	21.43	100.00	96.22
.792	3	277	280	21.43	100.00	96.22
.808	3	277	280	21.43	100.00	96.22
.825	3	277	280	21.43	100.00	96.22
.842	3	277	280	21.43	100.00	96.22
.858	3	277	280	21.43	100.00	96.22
.875	3	277	280	21.43	100.00	96.22
.892	2	277	279	14.29	100.00	95.88
.908	2	277	279	14.29	100.00	95.88
.925	2	277	279	14.29	100.00	95.88
.942	2	277	279	14.29	100.00	95.88
.958	2	277	279	14.29	100.00	95.88
.975	2	277	279	14.29	100.00	95.88
.992	2	277	279	14.29	100.00	95.88

TABLE 6.5

Risk Classifications

Classification	Cut-Off Point Range	Members of Risk Class
A	.000 - .008	0 Failed Banks 231 Solvent Banks
B	.0081 - .042	1 Failed Bank 22 Solvent Banks
C	.0421 - .175	1 Failed Bank 13 Solvent Banks
D	.1751 - .375	1 Failed Bank 6 Solvent Banks
E	.3756 - .492	1 Failed Bank 2 Solvent Banks
F	.4921 - 1.00	10 Failed Banks 3 Solvent Banks

TABLE 6.6

12 Bank Holdout Sample

Observation Failed	Solvent	Bank Name	Pred. Prob.	Risk Class
0	1	Akron State Bank	.00022	A
0	1	First National Bank of Windsor	.03100	B
0	1	The Crookville Bank	.00149	A
0	1	McIntosh County Bank	.00020	A
0	1	First National Bank of Lea	.00007	A
0	1	Republic Bank and Trust Co.	.00000	A
1	0	The Des Plaines Bank	.95837	F
1	0	Midtown National Bank	.56972	F
1	0	South Side Bank	.22773	D
1	0	Southwestern Bank	.75600	F
1	0	Northwest Commerce Bank	.60505	F
1	0	High Lakes Community Bank	.98514	F

NOTES

1. The random sample was chosen by selecting every 60th bank off the FDIC data tapes. The sample then is not truely random but does reflect objectiveness.

2. There are obvious problems with stepwise regressions. Normally, models should suggest the variables to be included. However, there exists no such model for the prediction of bank failure.   Stepwise procedures are common in the literature and are used to find those variables that best discriminate between failed and solvent banks.

3. The sample of 274 banks appears to be representative of the population of banks.   For example, of the 274 banks, 40 percent are members of the Federal Reserve system, 30 percent are national banks and 60 percent are nonmembers of the Federal Reserve system. This is extremely close to the population percentages of 39 percent members, 32 percent national, and 61 percent non-members (the FDIC Annual Report 1978).   The distribution of the size of banks in our sample, however, is not completely representative since our sample excludes U.S. banks with foreign offices.   Thus the very large U.S. banks, which usually have foreign offices are not represented.

4. Actually, there were 10 banks that failed in 1979. However, only 7 of them had the neccessary data qualifications for this study.

5. Our list of explanatory variables is limited and excludes some potentially significant variables, such as revenue from state and local obligations/total operating income. Exclusion of these variables is due to insufficient data for several observations.

6. Population data for a bank's respective county were taken from the 1980 United States Census survey.

7. Notice that the cut-off point range .492-1.00 could be broken down into smaller ranges for our classification purposes. However, we assume that banks with predicted probabilities of .492 or greater are potential failed banks and are therefore grouped together into the highest risk group, F.

8. Actually, 10 banks failed in 1981 but only 6 of these met the necessary data requirements for our study.

9. However, income per capita by county at the time of this study had not yet been made available by the United States 1980 census survey. Also there exists no reliable index of economic condition by county.

7

Conclusion

This study was undertaken to examine accident and bank insurance markets in the context of information problems, and to evaluate the effects of existing regulations. Information problems in these markets exist primarily because of the inabilities of market participants to accurately assess "risk," a crucial ingredient in the insurance process. Regulation has been justified in both markets for the same reason: to inhibit price wars and to protect firms from bankruptcy so they can keep their financial promises made to customers. The purpose of this study, then, is to assess how market participants respond to market information problems and existing regulations and to characterize market equilibrium.

The examinations reveal that information problems may significantly alter firm and customer behavior in the insurance process and thereby affect insurance market outcomes. For example, insurance firms operating in an informationally plagued market, may take advantage of consumer misinformation by altering the type of policies offered, their coverage levels, and the price charged for the insurance coverage offered. Further, insurance schemes and their regulations in both accident and bank insurance markets may adversely affect the market's way of dealing with information problems. For example, accident insurance regulation may impair a firm's ability to respond to and even to detect changing market conditions. And for bank insurance, the FDIC insurance scheme makes no effort at bank risk classification.

In Chapter 3, existing regulations in the accident insurance market are assessed, taking account of information problems. The analyses show that, besides creating higher

prices for insurance policies, rate regulation may alter a
market's policy offerings in that firms may switch from offering pooling contracts to offering separating contracts or vice
versa, depending on the riskiness composition of individuals in
the market. And under a prior-approval system, regulation
impairs a firm's ability to respond to and even to detect
changing market conditions, and so it results in less stable
insurance firm operations. Also, coverage restrictions may
indirectly force firms to drop their separating contracts in
favor of pooling contracts. It is also important to assess the
effects of consumer misinformation on market outcomes in the
context of informational asymmetries. The examinations reveal
that firms can take advantage of consumer misinformation by
altering the type of policies offered, their coverage levels,
and the price charged for the insurance coverage offered.
Finally, real world observations in the accident insurance
industry can be explained in terms of our analyses.

Chapter 4 examines how accident insurance firms respond
to market information problems by risk classification. The
chapter reveals that there is a bias in classifying individual
risk in that firm participation is more likely when the market
initially offers separating contracts than when the market
initially offers pooling contracts. The analysis also finds
that firms pass on the cost of classification only to the low-
risk group. And allowing for differing classification accuracies, from initial pooling contracts, inaccurate classification
results in less efficient market outcomes, while from initial
separating contracts, inaccurate classification results in
efficient market outcomes. Finally, depending on the level of
accuracy, bureau classification may offer pooling contracts
while independent classification offers separating contracts,
or vice versa.

In Chapter 5, bank insurance is examined in the context of
its information problems. The examinations reveal that the
presence of severe information problems may preclude a well
functioning competitive bank insurance market, and may ultimately lead to market failure. Today's bank insurance scheme,
a Federal Deposit Insurance Corporation (FDIC) regulatory
arrangement, is then assessed in the context of these information problems. Findings reveal that FDIC deposit
insurance results in big depositors partially insuring by purchasing a high-priced pooling contract, while small depositors
fully insure by purchasing a low-priced pooling contract. In
contrast to a competitive bank insurance market with asymmetric
information problems, FDIC insurance results in non-Pareto market outcomes. And FDIC insurance improves market outcomes only
in the case where a competitive bank insurance market exhibits
a dual information problem, i.e. both buyer and seller have
difficulty assessing the probability of bank failure. Also,
FDIC insurance may significantly disturb a bank's liability and
asset operations. In particular, the presence of FDIC

insurance might cause banks to take riskier positions on their efficient portfolio frontiers.

In Chapter 6, the possibility of commercial bank risk classification is empirically investigated. Logit analysis is performed on a sample of commercial banks consisting of failed commercial banks and a random sample of solvent commercial banks. The empirical findings indicate that financial ratios as well as other variables such as the number of bank branches, city vs. country banks, and whether a bank belongs to the Federal Reserve system are important predictors of bank failure. The model classifies the sample banks according to their predicted probabilities of failure. The model is shown to have good predictive ability by successfully testing it on a holdout sample.

This study's examinations suggest that government intervention in informationally imperfect markets, although intended to improve market outcomes and assure industry stability, is unsatisfactory and needs to be designed to take account of the market's information problems. Indeed, for the accident insurance market, a Federal Property-Liability Insurance Corporation (FPLIC) alternative is proposed to current insurance regulations. Under such a system, insurance firms would be required to join the FPLIC and pay premiums for insurance coverage. A FPLIC arrangement, then, would allow the competitive insurance market to operate freely in the pricing and marketing of its policies and to deal with market information problems, while assuring a financially sound industry through insurance coverage. And the FPLIC can also act as an information center for the property-liability industry by using its enormous data base to conduct insurance market research in an effort to improve the market's abilities to deal with information problems. And for the bank insurance market, it is proposed that the FDIC continue to insure all member banks, but with a modified payment system. A two-part tariff system is suggested where banks pay an initial payment for participating in the insurance process and then pay a premium for insurance coverage based on their riskiness. Under this proposed two-part premium, the FDIC will classify banks into their appropriate risk classes, which may help alleviate the market's information problems while assuring a financially sound banking industry through insurance coverage.

In summation, the presence of information problems and regulation in insurance markets makes it difficult for both buyer and seller to assess properly the type of product sold in the marketplace (i.e., insurance coverage) and thus alters buyer and seller behavior. And, in turn, this could lead to unnecessary product differentiation (i.e., differing separating and pooling policies, coverage levels, prices and risk classification). The government's role, aside from assuring industry stability should be as an information center (i.e., to provide information to buyers and sellers of insurance to help them define their product) so that the competitive insurance market can be free to allocate efficiently the marketing and selling of insurance.   And, finally, these analyses can be extended to examine other informationally plagued markets. For example, an application of these analyses to the labor market, as revealed in Miyazaki (75) and Spence (100), may improve our assessments of how minimum wage laws and other labor regulations affect labor market outcomes.

Bibliography

1. Akerlof, G. "Market For Lemons: Qualitative Uncertainty and the Market Mechanism," Quarterly Journal of Economics, August 1970.

2. Altman, E. "Financial Ratios, Discriminate Analysis and the Prediction of Corporate Bankruptcy," Journal of Finance, September 1968.

3. Altman, E. "Predicting Railroad Bankruptcies in America," The Bell Journal, Spring 1973.

4. Arrow, K. Essays in the Theory of Risk Bearing, Copy 1971 by Markham: Chicago.

5. Arrow, K. "Le Role des Valeurs Bousieres pour la Repartition la Meilleure des Risques," in International Colloquim on Econometrics, 1952. Paris: Centre National de la Recherche Scientifique, 1953.

6. Arrow, K. "The Role of Securities in the Optimal Allocation of Risk-Bearing," Review of Economic Studies, April 1964.

7. Arrow, K. "Uncertainty and the Welfare Economics of Medical Care," American Economic Review, December 1963.

8. Athearn, J. Risk and Insurance, Copy 1969 by Merideth Corp.

9. Averch, H. and Johnson, L. "Behavior of the Firm Under Regulatory constraint," American Economic Review, December 1962.

10. Barnett, R., Horvitz, P. and Silverberg, S. "Deposit Insurance: The Present System and some Alternatives," Banking Law Journal, April 1977.

11. Beaver, W. "Financial Ratios as Predictors of Failure, Empirical Research in Accounting: Selected Studies," Supplement to Journal of Accounting Research, Autumn 1966.

12. Beaver, W. "Market Prices, Financial Ratios, and the Prediction of Failure," Journal of Accounting Research, Autumn 1966.

13. Becker, F. and Ehrlich, I. "Market Insurance, Self Insurance, and Self Protection," Journal of Political-Economy, July 1972.

171

14. *Best's Aggregates and Averages*, Property and Liability Edition. New York: Alfred M. Best, Inc., published annually.

15. Blair, R. and Heggestande, A. "Bank Portfolio Regulation and the Probability of Bank Failure," *Journal of Money, Credit and Banking*, February 1978.

16. Blair, R. and Kenny, L.   *Microeconomics for Managerial Decision Making*, Copy 1982 by McGraw-Hill, Inc.

17. Bovenzi, J., Marino, J. and McFadden, F. "Commercial Bank Failure Prediction Models," *Economic Review*, Federal Reserve Bank of Atlanta, November 1983.

18. Brainard, C. and Carbine, S. "Price Variability in the Automobile Insurance Market," Bureau of Economics, Federal Trade Commission, August 1970.

19. Buser, S., Chen, A. and Kane, E. "Federal Deposit Insurance, Regulatory Policy, and Optimal Bank Capital," *The Journal of Finance*, March 1981.

20. Cook, P. and Graham, D. "The Demand for Insurance and Protection: The Case of Irreplaceable Commodities," *Quarterly Journal of Economics*, February 1977.

21. Crocker, K. "Mergers and Multiplant Economies with Private Information," Working Paper, University of Virginia, 1981.

22. Cumming, J. *An Econometric Model of the Life Insurance Sector of the U.S. Economy*, Copy 1975 by Lexington Books.

23. Cummins, J. et al. "Consumer Attitudes Toward Auto and Homeowners Insurance," Wharton School Department of Insurance Report, 1980.

24. Day, J. "Economic Regulation of Insurance in the United States," prepared for the Department of Transportation, 1970.

25. Debreu, G. *Theory of Value: An Axiomatic Analysis of Economic Equilibrium*. Copy 1959 by John Wiley: New York.

26. Diamond, P. "The Role of a Stock Market in a General Equilibrium Model with Technilogical Uncertainty," *American Economic Review*, September 1967.

27. Diamond, P. and Rothschild, M. Uncertainty in Economics, Copy 1978 by Academic Press, Inc.: New York.

28. Epps, W. "A General Mean-Variance Approximation to Expected Utility for Short Holding Periods," Working Paper, University of Virginia 1979.

29. Fama, E. Foundations of Finance, Copy 1976 by Basic Books: New York.

30. Federal Deposit Insurance Corporation 1980 Annual Report, Published by the Federal Deposit Insurance Corporation, Washington, D.C.

31. Federal Deposit Insurance Corporation," Deposit Insurance in a Changing Environment, published by the Federal Deposit Insurance Corporation, April 1983, Washington, D.C.

32. Federal Reserve Bulletin, "Statement on Proposed Changes in FDIC Insurance," May 1963.

33. Fisher, D. Money & Banking and Monetary Policy, Copy 1980 by Richard Irwin, Inc.

34. Friedman, M. and and Formuzis, P. "Bank Capital: The Deposit-Protection Incentive," Journal of Bank Research, Autumn 1975

35. Friedman, M. and Savage, L. "The Utility Analysis of Choices Involving Risks," Journal of Political Economy, August 1948.

36. Friedman, M. and Schwartz, A. A Monetary History of the United States: 1867-1960, Copy 1963 by Princeton University Press, Princeton, N.J.

37. Gibson, W. "Deposit Insurance in the United States: Evaluation and Reform," Journal of Financial and Quantitative Analysis, March 1972.

38. Gilbert, A. "Bank Failures and Public Policy," Federal Reserve Bank of St. Louis Review, November 1975.

39. Golembe, C. "The Deposit Insurance Legislation of 1933," Political Science Quarterely, June 1960.

40. Greene, M. Risk and Insurance, Copy 1977 by South-Western Publishing Co., Cincinnati, Ohio.

41. Grossman, H. "Adverse Selection, Dissembling, and Competitive Equilibrium," Working Paper, Brown University, 1976.

42. Grossman, S. "The Existence of Futures Market, Noisy Rational Expectations and Informational Externalities," Review of Economic Studies, October 1977.

43. Grossman, S. and Stiglitz, J. "Information and Competitive Price Systems," American Economic Review, May 1976.

44. Harris, M. and Townsend, R. "Resource Allocation Under Asymmetric Information," Econometrica, January 1981.

45. Herstein, I. and Milnor, J. "An Axiomatic Approach to Measurable Utility," Econometrica, April 1953.

46. Hill, R. "Profit Regulation in Property-Liability Insurance," The Bell Journal, Spring 1979.

47. Hirshleifer, J. and Riley, J. "The Analytics of Uncertainty and Information: An Expository Survey," Journal of Economic Literature, December 1979.

48. Horvitz, P. "Failures of Large Banks: Implications for Banking Supervision and Deposit Insurance," Journal of Financial and Quantitative Analysis, November 1975.

49. Hoy, M. "Categorizing Risks in the Insurance Industry," Quarterly Journal of Economics, MaY 1982.

50. Huebner, S., Black, K., and Cline, R. Property and Liabililty Insurance, Copy 1976 by Prentice-Hall, Engelwood Cliffs, New Jersey.

51. Jennrich, R. and Moore, R. "Maximum Likelihood Estimation by means of Non-Linear Least Squares," in Proceedings of the Statistical Computing Section of the American Statistical Association, 1975.

52. Johnson, B. "The Cross-Sectional Stability of Financial Ratio Patterns," Journal of Financial and Quantitative Analysis, December 1979.

53. Joskow, P. "Cartels, Competition and Regulation in the Property-Liability Insurance Industry," The Bell Journal, Autumn 1973.

54. Jovanovic, B. "Adverse Selection Under Symmetric Infor-

mation," Bell Laboratories and Columbia University Working Paper, December 1978.

55. Jovanovic, B. "Location in a New Market When Entrants have Private Information," Bell Laboratory Working Paper, 1979.

56. Karekan, J. and Wallace, N. "Deposit Insurance and Bank Regulation: A Partial-Equilibrium Exposition" Journal of Business, July 1978.

57. Kilhstrom, R. and Mirman, L. "Information and Market Equilibrium," The Bell Journal, Spring 1975.

58. Klein, M. "A Theory of the Banking Firm," Journal of Money, Credit and Banking, May 1971.

59. Kleindorfer, P. and Kunreuther, H. "Misinformation and Equilibrium in Insurance Markets," Working Paper, University of Pennsylvania, 1980.

60. Knight, F. Risk,Uncertainty and Profit, Copy 1921 by Hart, Schaffner and Marx: New York.

61. Koehn, M. Bankruptcy Risk in Financial Depository Intermediaries Copy 1979 by Lexington Books.

62. Kreps, C. and Wacht,R. " A More Constructive Role for Deposit Insurance," Journal of Finance, May 1971.

63. Kunreuther, H. et al., Disaster Insurance Protection: Public Policy Lessons, Copy 1978 by Wiley-Interscience, New York.

64. Leland, H. and Pyle, D. "Informational Asymmetries, Financial Structure and Financial Intermediation," Journal of Finance, May 1977.

65. Lorrie, S. and Hamilton, M. The Stock Market: Theories and Evidence, Copy 1973 by Irwin Inc.

66. Luce, D. and Raiffa, H. Games and Decisions, Copy 1957 by John Wiley and Sons: New York.

67. Lynch, M. "Comment on Munch and Smallwood," in Studies in Public Regulation, Edited by Gary Fromm, Copy 1981 by MIT Press, Cambridge, Mass.

68. MacAvoy, P. Edited: Federal- State Regulation of the Pricing and Marketing of Insurance, AEI Study, 1977.

69. Markowitz, H.   Portfolio Selection: Efficient Diversi-
     fication   of   Investments,   Cowles   Foundation   for
     Research in Economics, Yale University,   Monograph 16,
     Copy 1959 by John Wiley: New York.

70. Marschak, J. "Decision Making: Economic Aspects," Inter-
     national   Encyclopedia of the Social Sciences,   Copy
     1968 by Macmillan Free Press: New York.

71. Mayer, T. "A Graduated Deposit Insurance Plan," Review of
     Economics and Statistics, February 1965.

72. Mayer, T.   "Should Large Banks be Allowed to Fail?"
     Journal of Financial and Quantitative Analysis, Novem-
     ber 1975.

73. Meltzer, A. "Major Issues in the Regulation of Financial
     Institutions,"   Journal of Political Economy, August
     1976.

74. Merton, R. "An Analytic Derivation of the Cost of Deposit
     Insurance and Loan Guarantees: An Application of
     Modern Option Pricing Theory," Journal of Banking and
     Finance, June 1977.

75. Merton, R. "On the Cost of Deposit Insurance When There
     are Surveillance Costs," Journal of Business, July
     1978.

76. Meyer, P. and Pifer, H. "Prediction of Bank Failures,"
     Journal of Finance, September 1970.

77. Miyazaki, H. "The Rate Race and Internal Labor Markets,"
     The Bell Journal, Autumn 1977.

78. Mossin, J. "Aspects of Rational Insurance Purchasing,"
     Journal of Political Economy, July/August 1968.

79. Munch, P. and   Smallwood, D. "Theory   of Solvency
     Regulation in the Property and Casualty Insurance
     Industry," in Studies in Public Regulation edited by
     Gary Fromm, Copy 1981 by MIT Press, Cambridge,
     Massachusetts.

80. Munch, P. and Smallwood, D. "Solvency Regulation in the
     Property and Casualty Insurance Industry: Empirical
     Evidence," The Bell Journal, Spring 1980.

81. Muth, J. "Rational Expectations and the Theory of Price
     Movements," Econometrica, July 1961.

82. New York Insurance Department,Report to the Governor and
    State Legislature, "Cartels vs. Competition: A Criti-
    que of Insurance Price Regulation," 1975.

83. Pauly, M. "The Economics of Moral Hazard: Comment,"
    American Economic Review, June 1968.

84. Pauly, M. "Over Insurance and Public Provision of Insur-
    ance: The Roles of Moral Hazard and Adverse Selec-
    tion," Quarterly Journal of Economics, February 1974.

85. Pettway, R. and Sinkey, J. "Establishing On-Site Bank
    Examination Priorities: An Early-Warning System Using
    Accounting and Marketing Information," Journal of
    Finance, March 1980.

86. Prescott, E. and Townsend, R. "Equilibrium Under
    Uncertainty: Multi-Agent Statistical Decision
    Theory," in Studies in Bayesian Econometrics and
    Statistics in Honor of Harold Jeffreys, edited by
    Arnold Zellner, Copy 1978 by North-Holland Publishing
    Co., New York.

87. Prescott, E. and Visscher, M. "Sequential Location Among
    Firms with Foresight," The Bell Journal, Autumn 1977.

88. Randall, K. "The Federal Deposit Insurance Corporation:
    Regulatory Functions and Philosophy," Journal of Law
    and Contemporary Problems, Autumn 1966.

89. Riley, J. "Competitive Signaling," Journal of Economic
    Theory, April 1975.

90. Riley, J. "Informational Equilibrium" Econometrica, March
    1979.

91. Rose, P. and Scott, W. "Risk in Commercial Banking:
    Evidence from Post-war Failures," Southern Economic
    Journal, July 1978.

92. Rothschild, M. "Models of Market Organization with
    Imperfect Information: A Survey," Journal of Politi-
    cal Economy, December 1973.

93. Rothschild, M. and Stiglitz, J. "Equilibrium in Competi-
    tive Insurance Markets: An Essay on the Economics of
    Imperfect Information," Quarterly Journal of Econo
    mics, November 1976.

94. Saba, R. "An Alternative Theory of the Regulation of

Automobile   Insurance,"   Southern Economic Journal,
October 1978.

95. Salop, J. and Salop, S. "Self Selection and Turnover in
the Labor   Market," Quarterly Journal of Economics,
August 1976.

96. Scott, K. and Mayer, T. "Risk and Regulation in Banking:
Some Proposals for FDIC Reform," Stanford Law Review,
May 1971.

97. Sharpe, W. "Bank Capital Adequacy, Deposit Insurance and
Security   Values," Journal of Financial Quantitative
Analysis, November 1978.

98. Sinkey, J. "A Multivariate Statistical Analysis of the
Characteristics of Problem Banks," Journal of Finance,
March 1975.

99. Sinkey, J. "Identifying 'Problem' Banks," Journal of
Money, Credit and Banking, May 1978.

100. Sinkey, J. and Walker, D. "Problem Banks: Identification
and Characteristics," Journal of Bank Research, Spring
1975.

101. Smith, V. "Optimal Insurance Coverage," Journal of Political Economy, January/February 1968.

102. Spence, M. "Job Market Signaling," Quarterly Journal of
Economics, August 1973.

103. Spence, M. "Product Differentiation and Performance in
Insurance   Markets," Journal of Public Economics,
December 1978.

104   Spence, M. and Zeckhauser,R. "Insurance, Information
and Individual Action," American Economic Review, May
1971.

105. Stanford Research Institute, "The Role of Risk Classification in Property and Casualty Insurance: A Study of
the Risk Assessment Process," Final Report, 1976.

106. Stiglitz, J. "Monopoly,Non-Linear Pricing and Imperfect
Information: The Insurance Market," The Review of
Economic Studies, October 1977.

107. Theil, H. Principles of Econometrics, Copy 1971 by John
Wiley and Sons.

108. Van Horn, J. <u>Financial Management and Policy</u>, Copy 1971
      by Prentice-Hall.

109. Varian, H. <u>Micro-Economic Analysis</u>, Copy 1978 by Norton
      and Company Inc.

110. Varvel, W. "FDIC Policy Toward Bank Failures," <u>Economic
      Review</u>, Federal Reserve Bank of Richmond, September/
      October 1976.

111. Virginia Bureau of Insurance State Corporation Commission
      Report, "Competition in the Propertry and Casualty In-
      surance Industry: An Evaluation   of Alternative
      Methods of Rate Regulation," January 1978, Richmond,
      Virginia.

112. von Neumann, J. and Morgenstern, O. <u>Theory of Games and
      Economic Behavior</u>, Copy 1944 by Princeton University
      Press.

113. Wilson, C. "A Model of Insurance Markets with Incomplete
      Information," <u>Journal of Economic Theory</u>,   December
      1977.

114. Zeckhauser, R. "Medical Insurance: A Case Study of the
      Trade-off Between Risk Spreading   and Appropriate
      Incentives," <u>Journal of Economic Theory</u>, March 1970.

Index

administrative costs,
82–84
adverse selection,
3, 17, 18, 20, 32,
34, 40, 42, 54, 63,
66, 87, 88, 112
agency system, 3, 26
Akerlof, G. 32, 139
All-Industry Laws, 5
Arrow, K. 11, 12, 14, 32
asset restrictions, 129
asymmetric information:
defined, 17, 18, 125,
informational
asymmetries, 35, 38,
40, 59, 60,
75, 76, 87
automobile insurance,
63, 64,
66–67,
74, 139
Averch, H. 24

bank failures:
reasons, 136
Banking Act of 1933, 120
bank objective function,
125–126
bank portfolio:
return and risk, 129
determination, 132
bank risk characteristics,
see risk classification
Barnett, R. 28, 33,
Becker, G. 32
binary variable, see
dichotomous
dependent variable
Bovenzi, J. 144–145
Buser, J. 31, 33

C.C. Brown Goodness-of-Fit
Test, 148
Chen, A. 31, 33
Cook, P. 32
contingent-claim
model, 11

constant relative risk
aversion, 133
contract offer lines:
derivation, 80–81
Crocker, K. 32
Cummins, F. 56, 86

Debreu, G. 11, 12
deductible insurance
policies:
definition, 63;
offered by New York, 72;
similarities with
separating contracts, 63–67
Depository Monetary Control
Act of 1980, 125, 140
Diamond, P. 32
dichotomous dependent
variable, 143–145;
binary variable, 146–147
direct writing, 3
dual information
problem, 119

efficient portfolio
frontier,
125, 129, 132, 134, 140
Epps, W. 140
Erlich, I. 32
Expected Utility Hypothesis,
10, 11

Fama, E. 140
Federal Deposit Insurance
Corporation (FDIC):
impact in the R-S-W model,
120–123, 125;
insurance premium,
119–121, 123, 125–126,
133, 136–138, 139–140,
147, 154, 167–169
Federal Property-Liability
Insurance Corporation
(FPLIC), 77–78, 169
Federal Savings and Loan
Insurance Corporation
(FSLIC), 137

About the Author

DAVID A. LEREAH is a financial economist at the Federal Deposit Insurance Corporation. Until 1983 he was Assistant Professor of Economics at the Graduate School of Management, Rutgers University. His recent work has been involved with the analysis of the insurance and banking industries.

Dr. Lereah received a B.A. in economics and marketing from the American University, Washington D.C. and a Ph.D. in economics from the University of Virginia, Charlottesville, Virginia.